Understanding Language in Diverse Classrooms

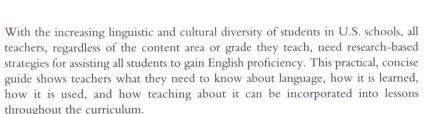

With the increasing linguistic and cultural diversity of students in U.S. schools, all teachers, regardless of the content area or grade they teach, need research-based strategies for assisting all students to gain English proficiency. This practical, concise guide shows teachers what they need to know about language, how it is learned, how it is used, and how teaching about it can be incorporated into lessons throughout the curriculum.

Understanding Language in Diverse Classrooms offers a model of how learning takes place and describes the critical role of teachers in that model. It includes comparison charts showing how some of the most common heritage languages represented among present-day students compare with English, and it provides examples of hands-on materials including checklists, rating scales, and sample lessons to help teachers prepare to teach all their students in diverse classrooms. Each chapter ends with questions to stimulate discussion and reflection on major chapter points, to enable readers to review and evaluate the information and then integrate it into their own practice.

Key features:

- A practical guide for all teachers about how to facilitate English proficiency as they teach their grade levels or content areas
- Critical information on languages and their relation to culture and on the nature of dual language learning
- Comparison charts showing how some of the most common heritage languages represented in American classrooms compare with English
- Checklists of practices to help teachers prepare for the challenge of diverse classrooms
- Hands-on materials, including sample lessons and suggested assessments, to assist in the teaching and evaluation of student learning

Marilyn Shatz is Adjunct Professor of Psychology, University of North Carolina Wilmington, and Professor Emerita, Psychology and Linguistics, University of Michigan.

Louise C. Wilkinson is Distinguished Professor of Education, Psychology, and Communication Sciences at Syracuse University.

Understanding Language in Diverse Classrooms

A Primer for All Teachers

Marilyn Shatz
Louise C. Wilkinson

Routledge
Taylor & Francis Group

NEW YORK AND LONDON

First published 2013
by Routledge
711 Third Avenue, New York, NY 10017

Simultaneously published in the UK
by Routledge
2 Park Square, Milton Park, Abingdon, Oxon OX14 4RN

Routledge is an imprint of the Taylor & Francis Group, an informa business

Library of Congress Cataloging in Publication Data
A catalog record has been requested for this book

ISBN: 978-0-415-89443-2 (hbk)
ISBN: 978-0-415-89444-9 (pbk)
ISBN: 978-0-203-81351-5 (ebk)

Typeset in Bembo and Gill Sans
by Florence Production Ltd, Stoodleigh, Devon

SUSTAINABLE
FORESTRY
INITIATIVE

Certified Sourcing
www.sfiprogram.org
SFI-00555
The SFI label applies to the text stock.

Printed and bound in the United States of America by
Walsworth Publishing Company, Marceline, MO.

To our teachers

Contents

Preface

This is the second book we have written together. The first, *The education of English language learners* (Shatz & Wilkinson, 2010), was, as is this one, a book for practicing teachers and those who are preparing to teach in US public schools. However, the first book was an edited volume, with its chapters written by experts who summarized the best of current education research. Although we learned much from those chapters, we felt that there was a need for something still more practical, both for pre-service teachers and teachers who may have been away from their initial preparation for some time and are in need of professional re-invigoration. Thus, using our decades of experience as educators in language, psychology, and communication, we set out to fill that need.

We had two goals in preparing this book. The first was to redress insufficiencies of educator preparation by providing the critical information on languages, their speakers, and their relationships to culture that is necessary for understanding today's diverse students. Despite repeated calls for more extensive preparation of teachers in the area of language and diversity (e.g., Wong Fillmore & Snow, 2000), many of the teachers in today's schools are under-prepared to deal with the range of background languages and cultures present-day students bring to their classrooms. We believe part of the reason for this lack of preparation is that relevant information about language and its use (not just teaching English as a Second Language [ESL]) is not readily accessible to all teachers. In Part I of our book, we offer such information.

The second goal was to offer all teachers suggestions for incorporating such knowledge of language diversity into their plans for educating students from varied backgrounds. We intend our book to be a practical guide for content area teachers about how to teach language/literacy in their subject matter to all students. It includes hands-on materials to help teachers both understand language and address English Language Learner (ELL) students' challenges in learning English. Our aim is to include easily accessible professional development activities that demonstrate the effectiveness of teaching language at the same time as teaching the content areas of K–12 grades.

Our volume is also timely because it directly addresses two trends characterizing contemporary education in the US at the beginning of the 21st century: 1) the achievement gap among students, and 2) the emphasis on accountability for public education. Both of these trends constrain the character of current teacher preparation and continuing professional development. Regarding 2), "Public education is on everyone's mind these days" (Tamir, 2011, p. 395), from members of the US Congress to Wall Street to the US Secretary of Education to teachers, parents, and students. Because education is recognized as the means by which generations of Americans have been able to better themselves, we all have a vested interest in improving our education system for every student. The American dream has been nurtured in US classrooms from the earliest preschool years. Despite budgetary constraints, teachers are expected to find ways to keep that dream alive.

As for 1), perhaps the most intractable problem in US education is the achievement gap that exists between groups of children who differ on home language, socio-economic status, race, or ethnicity. Long-standing gaps for ELLs, for example, appear early and become amplified as students progress from first grade through high school. Their negative consequences extend well past high school to higher education. And the widening gaps continue far beyond higher education, eventually leading to a decline in economic mobility. The influence of the gaps goes beyond the income ladder: poor school outcomes for ELLs (e.g., low literacy and graduation rates) have also been associated with poor health literacy, that is, the capacity to deal adequately with a range of health issues, resulting in a variety of health-related problems (Wolf, et al., 2009). This association bodes ill for future health care expenses.

New data from the 2010 Census point up the significance of the achievement gaps. Overall, as the US population growth rate slows, Hispanics account for more than 50 percent of the total population growth in the first decade of the 21st century (Humes, Jones, & Ramirez, 2011). Thus, Hispanic population growth continues to drive the growth in the country's racial and ethnic diversity. In addition, the Asian population also increased significantly. Four states (California, Hawaii, New Mexico, and Texas), in addition to the District of Columbia, are now "majority-minority" (Humes, Jones, & Ramirez, 2011, p. 19), meaning that the formerly non-white minority now exceeds 50 percent of the population; this trend is expected to expand even more in the south and west in the current decade. These demographic factors have considerable bearing on the achievement gaps confronting the US.

Our view on the direction for future policy-driven educational practice for ELLs is clear: we believe that it is essential for all teachers to know about language, language diversity, and what students must deal with when they are expected to learn both English and content area knowledge at the same time. Our book is designed to help teachers not well-versed in these issues to gain such knowledge. Regardless of the future direction of federal policy, all teachers handling any grade or subject area need to use such knowledge to embed information about English language in their plans for content area lessons.

We believe that, unless this is done, the statistics on the achievement gaps will not improve.

How This Book is Organized

Our book is organized into two parts. In Part I, we offer the kind of straight-forward information about language that most teachers have not had access to. Chapter 1 expands on the importance of knowledge about languages for teachers, and we briefly introduce the set of tools we will offer in Part II to help them use that knowledge in the classroom. In Chapters 2–4, we describe what human language and its learners are like, illustrate how human languages can be both similar and different, discuss how languages are related to cultures and to speakers, and report how language competence impacts learning by bilinguals.

Part II shows how teachers of all levels and content areas can bring their new knowledge about diverse languages and their speakers into the classroom to guide their students to success. Chapter 5 describes how to use checklists and rating scales to monitor teacher behavior and student progress in the classroom. Chapter 6 compares the characteristics of eight languages commonly found in US schools to those of English and shows how to use such comparisons to help identify challenges ELLs face as they learn English. Chapter 7 provides examples of how to embed language learning in content lessons, as well as how to engage in supportive discourse with students. Chapter 8 offers some suggestions for how classroom teachers can help in the assessment of ELL students to identify the range and types of challenges they face with either language or content.

To aid understanding and to offer opportunities for discussion and professional development, discussion questions are included at the end of each chapter. Also, we have provided two appendices that present lists for teachers to use to find additional support. Appendix A is a list of selected web sites we think are well designed, relatively easy to use, and full of information about languages and teaching. Appendix B is a short list of books for further reading on topics covered in the book. Finally, although we minimized technical terminology throughout and defined what we needed to use *in situ*, we have added for convenience a glossary of terms.

We conclude this preface by noting that the challenges presented by learning a second language as the language of instruction, at the same time as content is to be mastered, are not unique to learning English in the US. Levy (2011), an American journalist posted in Moscow, recounts the experiences of his three children when they attended a local school in Moscow, where Russian was the primary language of instruction. None of the children had studied Russian; it was total immersion. Many of the experiences that he described are similar to those of ELLs in the US who attend classes where English is the language of instruction. Levy's children were alienated and fearful at first, finding themselves bewildered and isolated; they were teased by other children. One day the school's English teacher presented a lesson completely in English so that the other students would understand how difficult it was for the Levy children. One Russian student "was so tormented trying to follow along that he burst into tears." The challenges for the Levy family were not limited to the three siblings alone. At one point, after a lengthy discussion with several of the teachers, the children's mother walked out of the school nearly in tears. Although she, too, was studying Russian, she soon became aware that she had failed to comprehend what the teachers were telling her, and asked herself, "How can you help your children when you can barely communicate with their teachers?" The Levy children did eventually feel good about school and speaking/learning in Russian, and they did learn content as well prior to their return to the US. Levy makes this key point: it took very understanding and skilled teachers and the eventual support from other students over time for his children to settle in and learn in their Moscow classrooms.

Acknowledgments

Each author contributed equally to this volume, and we take joint responsibility for what we say here.

We thank members of the University of Michigan linguistics community: Erica Beck, Patrice Beddor, Marlyse Baptista, Tridha Chatterjee, Steve Dworkin, Judy Dyer, Ioulia Kovelman, Harim Kwon, and Xinting Zhang gave valuable advice on language features and helped construct the Language Comparison Charts and/or the paragraphs about the languages in Chapter 6, as did Martha Ratliff of Wayne State University and Aysa Pereltsvaig of Stanford University. Sarah Thomason and Judy Dyer both offered useful references on language typology and language learning. Several people at the Faculty Exploratory at the University of Michigan Hatcher Library were indispensable in helping with the execution of the book cover design: Laurie Sutch, Peggah Ghoreishi, Sharona Ginsberg, and Jonathan Rodgers.

We are grateful to all those who read earlier versions of our manuscript. Louise Wilkinson's students at Syracuse University made suggestions and gave frank appraisals that were enormously helpful as we worked to complete the book. Robin Danzak of the University of South Florida, Elaine McNulty of the University of Michigan, and Lorrie Verplaetse of Southern Connecticut State University made constructive criticisms on the penultimate manuscript; their comments helped us improve the final version. Of course, all remaining faults are ours.

We thank our editor, Naomi Silverman of Routledge–Taylor & Francis; her suggestions and support throughout our year of writing were tremendously helpful and are greatly appreciated. Finally, we thank our husbands, Richard and Alex, who have cheerfully supported us throughout this exciting and, at times, arduous process.

Part I

Language and Languages

Chapter 1

Introduction

Why All Teachers Need to Know About Language

Humans are good language learners. Typical 4-year-olds are adept enough in their native language to use it to interact successfully with both parents and playmates across a host of social situations. And they do so without the laborious training it takes to get a chimp or a parrot to learn only a tiny fraction of what constitutes knowledge of human language. According to folk wisdom, children even pick up a second language with apparent ease if immersed in it at a young age. Yet, when it comes to schooling, language can be the stumbling block to learning for an increasingly large percentage of the population. Why? Our answer is two-fold: 1) folk wisdom ignores the complexities inherent in the task of acquiring and using language, and 2) all teachers must be equipped with knowledge about those complexities in order to foster academic success.

Schools have a language in which the tasks of teaching and learning are carried out. It is more complex and often more precise than social, or everyday, language. In the US, that school language is a particular variety of English labeled *Academic English* (Wilkinson & Silliman, 2008, 2010, & 2012). Over the years, the gap between everyday and academic language has grown. Moreover, an increasingly diverse student population from many different language and cultural backgrounds may not be proficient enough even in everyday English to cope with the academic variant found in schools (Danzak, Wilkinson, & Silliman, 2012). This can be true not just for young children but for older ones as well. In any level classroom, there may be students with a range of English and schooling experiences, some with everyday English and education elsewhere, some with one or the other, and some with neither (Silliman & Wilkinson, 2010). While all teachers are increasingly held to account for the success of all their students, few educators have been prepared by their initial preparation to understand how or why students from such varied backgrounds may have so much difficulty with instruction conducted in Academic English.

All teachers need to recognize that a key challenge in content learning is for students to move from everyday, informal ways of construing and representing knowledge into the technical and academic ways that are necessary for disciplinary learning in all subjects. Each content area has its own vocabulary and its own modes of expression for argument and persuasion. Students, especially English Language Learners (ELLs), will learn disciplinary content only if they understand its particular language. Content area teachers are responsible for helping them use that language appropriately.

Why is learning about language diversity and how to use knowledge about it in the classroom now so important for all teachers? It is not news that language is crucial for learning in school. For decades, teachers have been giving oral instructions and students have been reading texts, writing essays, and taking tests. Whether learning to read, do an experiment, or solve an equation, students have used language to comprehend what they were being taught and to express what they have learned. It has always been important that students attain competence in the language of schooling, Academic English.

However, it is news that, increasingly, students of all ages come to school underprepared to deal with Academic English. The language diversity of students in American public schools continues to grow. In 2009, more than 20 percent of the student population in American schools did not have English as their home language (Aud, *et al.*, 2011). Many of these students are classified as ELLs; that is, they do not have adequate English language skills for schooling in English; the numbers increase yearly. Although children from Spanish-speaking backgrounds make up a large part of the ELL (or Dual Language Learner [DLL], or Limited English Proficiency [LEP]—as they are sometimes called) population, they are not the only ones. There is so much language diversity among students now that the school web sites of many large cities in the US often list the major languages represented in their districts. Moreover, for a given language, for example Spanish, there can be a number of different regional dialects or varieties found in the language backgrounds of students in US classrooms. Even for English, there are many varieties in classrooms across the country, from regional dialects to African American Vernacular English. In sum, the language diversity in almost any classroom is staggering.

How to meet the needs of such a diverse student population? US schools have addressed that question largely by introducing cadres of experts to deal with it. There are now special classes for ELLs, with English as a Second Language (ESL) expert teachers, reading teachers, and expert speech therapists (Danzak, Wilkinson, & Silliman, 2012). Such additional expert assistance may be extremely useful, but it is not enough. ELLs are often put in special classes or pulled out of regular classes for additional services. There is a limit to how much this can be done. As much as they might need special help, ELL students also need to spend time in regular classrooms with content teachers who are expert in the particular language of science and math. Moreover, they need to practice what they learn in class with peers who speak Standard English, and they need the opportunity to compete or cooperate with them in regular classrooms. What, then, is the solution—one that allows for an integrated schooling experience for all students and yet addresses the challenges of reaching a diverse student population for the teacher?

We propose not to do away with expert assistance but additionally to give all teachers, regardless of the grade or content area they teach, the tools they must have to address adequately the language needs of the varied students they teach. Then, even though some ELLs may spend a part of the day in extra language instruction, all students will participate in regular classrooms and benefit from all teachers more knowledgeably addressing the language demands of their topics. ESL teachers should be seen as more of a resource and advocate for the ELL student than as a substitute for content teachers.

Below we expand on our two-part plan for this book: First, we describe the kind of information about language that most teachers have not previously had access to. Second, we offer suggestions on how teachers can use their new knowledge to improve their instruction to students who need to acquire Academic English language skills. For more on Academic English and the need for students to learn it, see Chapter 7 (this volume) and Wilkinson & Silliman, 2008, 2010, & 2012.

What Teachers Need to Know about Language

Although teachers recognize the importance of language skills for learning, they typically have had little education into the nature of languages, the acquisition of them, or the many ways languages relate to cognitive or social development. Moreover, there has been little attention paid to whether and how ELLs or DLLs are different from monolingual learners. Because almost all of us have reached an everyday conversational competence in our native languages before we even enter school, we tend to discount the magnitude of that first-language acquisition accomplishment and, moreover, to assume that further learning in language will be as apparently effortless. Recent research in psychology, linguistics, and education tells us, however, that while humans are prepared to learn and use language, the actual learning and ultimate uses of language are anything but simple. This is especially true of users of more than one language (see, for example, Hoff & Shatz, 2007).

Importantly, you do not have to learn another language or become an expert in linguistics, the formal study of languages, to learn what you as a teacher need to know in order to deal with the increased language diversity in your classroom. In the chapters in Part I, to give you a better appreciation of language and language learning, we plainly describe levels of language analysis, discuss how languages can differ, show how language development relates to social and cognitive development, and discuss how being an ELL or DLL can affect the educational process.

We ground our approach to language learning in classrooms in our training in developmental psychology and discourse analysis. We offer two constructs, *bootstrapping* and *discourse scaffolding*, that complement each other to present a picture of learning analogous to what goes on between caregiver and young child. Learning cannot progress without the interactive involvement of both learner and caregiver or teacher. The first construct, *bootstrapping*, focuses on children as learners, who draw on whatever their level of social, cognitive, and language experience in order to learn more. The second construct, *discourse scaffolding*, refers to the methods by which the caregiver or teacher facilitates and guides the child's progress by using language supports to help the child take the next steps toward knowledge. Learning from others via language is a hallmark of human development, both for a toddler being socialized into a language community and for a student in a US classroom. All teachers need to know how to use language to provide scaffolds for all their students, including ELLs.

How Teachers Can Use Their Knowledge of Language(s)

Because teachers already have so many educational and administrative tasks, we offer several devices to help them utilize their new knowledge. In Chapters 5–7 in Part II, we provide checklists, rating scales, language comparison charts, and age-based suggestions for including language learning in lessons, all designed as tools to help teachers manage the task of making their instructional plan responsive to the particular language needs of the varied students in their classrooms. In Chapter 8, we show how teachers can contribute to the language ability assessments of their students.

Checklists and Rating Scales

People make errors, their memories can fail them, and they can be disorganized. To help counter such tendencies, checklists have been employed in many enterprises. One example is their use in airplane cockpits before takeoff (Gawande, 2010). In Chapter 5, we offer checklists and rating scales to help teachers organize and keep track of the language backgrounds of the students in their classrooms, to identify sources of assistance for them, to help monitor their own communication with students and their parents, and to track the strategies they use to facilitate progress in learning.

Comparison Charts

One of the most difficult jobs for teachers, once they know their students' language backgrounds, is to identify where and why students may have problems learning English. Without requiring teachers to have proficiency in another language, our language charts show how many common difficulties result from clear differences between English and other languages, and how these differences may impact a particular aspect of learning, e.g., spelling of English words. Teachers can use the charts in Chapter 6 to examine some of the most common home languages represented in American schools today and see how they compare with English in various ways (e.g., major sound differences). Then they can see how those differences may impact a student's educational performance. They can also use the list of comparative features to make their own charts of languages represented in their classrooms but not in our book. Wikipedia and other web sources with information on languages (see Appendix A) should be helpful for such activities.

Language-Savvy Lessons and Assessment

Ultimately teachers are responsible for creating lessons that help children learn and eventually show what they have learned on evaluations. Based on information about innovative and successful classroom practices, we offer in Chapter 7 suggestions for both primary and secondary level teachers on how information about Academic English can be woven into lessons at any grade level and any topic. In addition, we provide some case studies illustrating successful methods. Chapter 8 is dedicated to an overview and application of assessment practices for ELLs. Our hope is that such suggestions and case studies will stimulate discussion and sharing among all teachers about such practices.

Additional Aids

Finally, we provide in two appendices sets of sources that include not only books expanding on topics in our volume, but also web sites we have found that seem especially well-designed and potentially useful for teachers. The web sites in Appendix A offer information about a wide variety of languages and even pronunciations of simple words. There are also sites that summarize recent research on young ELLs and offer suggestions and tools for teaching ELLs. In Appendix B, teachers who want to know more about languages, language development, or ELL or bilingual students can find books on those topics, as well as a range of recent books with chapters by experts on teaching.

Summary

We have made a case for all teachers needing to know about language in order to face the challenges of teaching the increasingly large numbers of students in US classrooms who need extra Academic English support. Central to our argument is our learning model, which uses the ideas of bootstrapping and discourse scaffolding as complementary processes that all students and teachers need to engage in if learning is to proceed. To assist teachers in their roles in the learning process, we will offer in the following chapters further discussion of language, types of languages, and characteristics of language learners, including bilinguals. We will go on to suggest how teachers can use checklists and language comparison charts, and we offer some examples of language-rich lessons as well as suggestions for assessment, additional readings, and useful web sites.

Discussion Questions

- Why should all content teachers know about language?
- What is every teacher's role in teaching ELLs?
- How can teachers use their knowledge of language to best assist ELL students to learn?

Chapter 2

Language and Its Speakers

What is Language?

How would you respond to the question, "What is language?" One answer (found in a dictionary) is "any means of expression or communication, as gestures, signs, animal sounds, etc." This answer is problematic. What about the barking of a dog, the purring of a cat, the crying of an infant? Many signs or signals convey information to us, but not all are language: indeed, the word *infant* comes from the Latin, meaning *having no language.*

Some of us have been privileged as caregivers to watch infants, from birth to three or four years of age, become language-using members of a community, able to persuade, joke, and argue. The apparent ease with which children attain so much skill in so short a time can be misleading: we are beguiled into thinking that acquiring language and how to use it in varied social settings is easy. Language acquisition may be natural—almost all children growing up in a wide variety of cultures and circumstances acquire language—but it cannot be said to be a simple process. After many decades of research, there is still controversy over how language is acquired (see Shatz, 2007a). Moreover, not even the brightest of non-human animals can do what toddlers do seemingly without training (Penn, Holyoak, & Povinelli, 2008). Animals, of course, have their own ways of communicating, and we have learned in recent years that such systems are often more complicated than we previously thought. Still, to date, no other species' communication system has been shown to approach human language in complexity or productive potential. And, no non-human animal has yet developed anything like full-blown human language abilities. So what is it that makes us human animals and our language different?

Language—at least human language—is more than conveying meaning through signs or sounds. It is an orderly system that allows for infinite productivity, that is, an unbounded variety of expressions. A simple instance of productivity involves continuing to add another noun with *and* to the subject of a sentence, e.g., "I like peaches," "Richard and I like peaches," "Richard and Louise and I like peaches," "Richard and Louise and Alex and I like peaches," etc. There are many other ways to be productive, for example, "I like peaches and bananas." Or, "I like sweet peaches." Yet, there are constraints on what is acceptable variation. For example, speakers of English would not say, "Peaches like I," or "I-s like peach." The point is that knowing a language means knowing how to create an infinite variety of expressions that follow the constraints or rules of that language.

Languages have traditionally been analyzed into various parts: sound systems (phonology), meaning systems (semantics), and systems for combining language units are traditionally divided into the studies of how words are structured (morphology) and how words are combined into the larger units of sentences (syntax). But such distinctions by themselves do not capture the full richness and subtlety of human languages, which use features like focus and stress to add to a speaker's intended meaning. For example, in English, when we say, "John kissed Mary," we place our focus on John. Saying "Mary kissed John" places our focus on Mary. "The BALL (stressed) went into the street" might answer the question, "What went into the street?" whereas "The ball went into the STREET" would answer, "Where did the ball go?" Learning how and when to utilize such features of meaning are part of acquiring a language for a human child.

Add to this already complex, multi-channel system, the pragmatics of language use for social purposes: knowing when to talk and when to be silent, how to argue, promise, convince, deceive, and placate. People use language not only to communicate facts or experiences to one another but also to convey emotions and beliefs. They also use it to enjoy pastimes such as reading, watching a play or movie, or doing a crossword puzzle. Despite the importance of graphics in the world of the internet, even the iTunes store has a separate category for word games. Language is the bedrock on which human culture is founded; it is the medium of politics, religion, and education. So, human language has multiple uses and multiple purposes. Without access to a culture through its language, a person can be marginalized and even isolated.

On Development: Human Learning

Many living creatures are born with both emotions and learning abilities. Experience with our pets confirms this. From birds to dogs, our pets demonstrate through their actions their affection for us, as well as their annoyance about being left alone. Animals discriminate sounds well, and they are biologically prepared to acquire the varied songs and noises of their species. When we domesticate animals, we take them from their natural social environment and immerse them in a human one, where we turn whatever proclivities they have for learning and emotional expression to our own purposes. For example, we train them to respond differentially to word commands and to tones of voice. We accomplish this best when we start with a young animal and engage it with human guidelines for its behavior. The saying, "You can't teach an old dog new tricks," is founded on this fact. However, human language in all its richness is beyond the ken of even a chimpanzee raised from infancy in a human household (Terrace, *et al.*, 1979).

On the one hand, like other animals, human babies have emotions and an ability to learn. On the other hand, they do not have to be especially trained in language; they are biologically prepared to develop in a human social environment, and so all their proclivities, supported by that natural environment, can be put to the task of acquiring language very early. Even *in utero*, near-term fetuses regularly exposed to sounds of human language show evidence of learning about pitch, rhythm and stress. Using behavioral techniques adapted for neonates, researchers have shown that 2-day-old infants prefer to hear their native language (i.e., the language of their mothers) over one with a different rhythmic pattern. (See Conboy, 2010, for a review.) Research on the amount and kind of language that infants hear has shown that speech surrounds them in all contexts of care. Caregivers tend to produce slower, higher-pitched, and better articulated speech to infants; higher economic groups tend to produce more of it (Hoff, 2009). Thus, infants have a broad data set upon which to base their learning. And learn they do. By one year of age, with no formal training, they not only recognize their own names and those of familiar others, but also they can understand other words and some aspects of grammar, they can segment words in fluent speech, and they may even already be producing a few words (see Hoff, *op. cit.*). One ability that has been shown to facilitate such accomplishments is the statistical analysis of regularities in the speech stream (Saffran & Thiessen, 2007). Another factor may be motivation: infants want to be like those around them, full-fledged members of their social group, and they practice at becoming such. Language practice is a well-documented phenomenon (Weir, 1962; Kuczaj, 1983; Shatz & Ebeling, 1991). We have observed a 6-month-old boy practicing hand gestures that his father regularly made when he talked, and a toddler, bringing a crossword puzzle to his avid puzzler mother, saying, "teach me, teach me" (Shatz, 1994).

The question of what if anything is unique about innate human abilities does not yet have a final answer, although surely there is at least one. (See Penn, Holyoak, & Povinelli, 2008, for a well-argued proposal.) However, some abilities that infants bring to language learning have been shown to be neither unique to language learning nor unique to humans. Infants attend to regularities for all sorts of category learning. Other animals have mature auditory systems at birth and can also recognize statistical regularities or patterns, although the specific characteristics of such abilities seem geared to phenomena likely to be found in the natural environment of their own species. The combination of a language-rich environment and a flexible and rich set of infant abilities allows the human infant to get a foothold into language. From there, children can bootstrap their partial knowledge with encouragement and interaction from a genial community.

Bootstrapping

Bootstrapping labels the developing child's use of partial knowledge or skill in an area so as to acquire more, or to use knowledge from one area to help master another. We can all think of examples of children (and even adults) using this strategy not only to extend their knowledge but also to produce at least partially appropriate behavior. For example, young language-learners use their limited language skills to learn more about language and how to interact in conversations (Shatz, 1987, 1994). They may know that questions often require a verbal answer, but they may not distinguish well among the intent of questions and may have only a limited range of responses that they use in all contexts. So, toddlers may answer "no" to "Do you want milk or juice?" or to "Do you want a cookie?" even while reaching for one (Shatz & McCloskey, 1984). Their responses, although not fully appropriate, are at least verbal ones, and such responses tend to result in caregivers continuing to talk in order to clarify or expand on them. Thereby, children get still more language from their interlocutors. (See Shatz, 1987, on children's elicitation operations.) Also, while caregivers often complain about the high frequency of young children's "why" questions, this is evidence that children both practice new-found language skills and use them to get still more information from their caregivers.

The bootstrapping model of development follows in the Piagetian tradition of child constructivism in cognitive development. Bootstrapping theory extends the notion of constructivism beyond cognitive development by emphasizing that children do not acquire language, social behavior, and cognitive understandings separately. However, instead of an underlying logic that governs all domains, bootstrapping theory proposes that, using experiences in their social environment, children actively influence their own development by inter-relating their various levels of understanding in all three realms, using knowledge in one domain to help learn in another.

To bootstrap, children need relevant language input from caregivers and relevant feedback on their behaviors, as well as adept models to observe. Thus, the theory is akin also to Vygotsky's work (1978), which championed the value of social interaction with adults meeting children in their "zone of proximal development." Vygotsky (1978) pointed out that children internalize the thinking and language patterns of more proficient speakers, and that this happens most efficiently when new language and concepts are just above the students' current levels of proficiency, or their "zone of proximal development." His insights provided a theoretical foundation for Bruner's (1986) studies of children's language and cognitive development. Bruner described children's shared learning experiences with the term *scaffolding*, which has since become a popular metaphor for the apprenticeship style of supporting children's learning. Scaffolding is the complement to bootstrapping: primary caregivers do it when they expand on their toddlers' limited language (Nelson, *et al.*, 1984), for example saying, "Yes, the ball is red", when their child exclaims, "Wed!"

In Chapter 7, we discuss in more detail the subject of discourse scaffolding for teachers.

Implications of the Bootstrapping Model of Development for Education

Although the bootstrapping model is based largely on evidence from toddlers, research suggests that the model applies to older children too. One of us had asked a preschooler, "How long should I cook this egg?" and was told, "Ten months" (Shatz, 1994). Further systematic investigation revealed that even older children often responded similarly to questions about time, using only partial knowledge to answer with appropriate (i.e., using a time word) but incorrect answers (Shatz, et al., 2010). Moreover, there is every reason to think bootstrapping holds for all children, second language learners as well as first. For example, regardless of race or ethnicity, children living in poverty who, for whatever reason, tend to be deficient in language skills also show deficits in cognitive and social skills. (See Nelson, et al., 2011, for a review.) And, as noted above, Bruner showed how scaffolded learning experiences influenced language and cognitive development. These findings support the claims 1) that even older children use partial knowledge to talk about abstract categories like time, 2) that levels of knowledge in one area can affect levels of knowledge in another, and 3) that social support is central to learning.

Language is pervasive. It impacts virtually every aspect of cognitive and social life. Very early in life it becomes a primary means by which children gain knowledge about themselves and their social, cultural, and physical worlds. Without competence in language, they are greatly limited in how they can learn from others. The spontaneous creation and use of home sign systems in families with deaf children attests not only to the natural propensity of humans to communicate through language, but also to the central role language plays in child development (Goldin-Meadow, 2003; Haviland, 2011).

There are several implications of this view of development, both for an understanding of student language learners and for teacher–student relations.

1. Learning a new language is not just a matter of learning a new vocabulary and set of grammatical rules. It involves learning new ways of speaking, interacting, and thinking. This is especially true when the new language is to be used in a new social setting such as school.

2. Because the use of language to learn more begins so early, even children at the start of schooling already bring with them a background in the language practices of their home communities and cultures. The longer they have been exposed to those practices, the more organized and codified their socio-linguistic knowledge will have become and the more they will need to learn and understand how those practices impact new experiences.

3.   The task of helping an English Language Learner (ELL) adapt to the use of
language in the classroom cannot be shouldered only by special teachers of
the language. Every teacher of any content area who has ELLs in his or her
classroom needs to understand how to help the students bootstrap; that is,
how to use the knowledge they already have to learn more.

4.   Teachers need to encourage students to express partial knowledge that can
be used to help them discover the relation between what is already known
and what is to be learned. That is, teachers need to *scaffold* for their students,
by expanding on their partial or incomplete knowledge and by showing
how it may be similar to or different from what is to be learned. Also,
teachers have to recognize possible difficulties in adapting to new rules of
use for newly acquired knowledge.

None of this is an easy task for any teacher. But, armed with knowledge of
how the development of a child proceeds via language interactions with a
patient adult, all teachers have the power to engage their ELL students
successfully.

Language, Cognition, and Social Skill

There are obvious ways to relate language to cognitive and social skills when
considering the bases of behavior. For example, language and cognitive skills
function together when vocabulary and grammatical skills work with memory,
reasoning, and organizational skills to create clear expressions of one's thoughts.
Language and social skills are both utilized in play settings with other children;
even preschoolers tend to avoid children who are deficient in one or the other,
suggesting that acceptable behavior depends on both.

A less obvious and even more basic sort of relation between language and
cognitive and social skills involves brain wiring. The brain is continually wiring
(and rewiring) itself as a consequence of its experiences. In the brain, the rich
get richer: parts that become highly inter-connected and frequently accessed
become still easier to use—this is what learning (and over-learning) is all about
and why practice is so helpful for learning. Language is an excellent tool for
facilitating the making of connections between parts of the brain. Family talk
about internal states such as emotions and beliefs facilitates preschoolers'
understandings of others (Dunn, *et al.*, 1991), and language, it has been argued,
is crucial to bridging the gap between simple arithmetic understandings that all
animals share and the deeper mathematical ones humans develop (Spelke, 2003).
Language, then, is both an object of learning and a tool for learning, not only
for more language but also for social and cognitive knowledge as well (Shatz,
2007b).

Experiences with language influence the brain's wiring very early, even in
pre-linguistic infants. As we will see in Chapter 3, the influence can result

in general consequences for cognitive and social behavioral development. Moreover, how very young children develop even fundamental concepts like spatial relations can be influenced by the language they hear as they organize their understandings of the physical world and how those relate to language. For example, consider the English word *in*. We use it to describe both putting an apple in a bowl and a hand in a glove, without consideration of degree of fit, whereas the Korean language takes account of that spatial relation in its vocabulary (Bowerman & Choi, 2001).

The direction of influence is not all one-way, however. Not only does language influence social and cognitive development, but also social and cognitive factors can influence language development. Because humans are social creatures and language very likely evolved in the service of communication, babies in normal environments seem to have little problem being motivated to acquire it, and they learn rules of its use at home simultaneously with learning vocabulary and grammar. Moreover, it is common knowledge that children can acquire a second language quite readily in a new social setting. All children, whether native speakers or not, have to learn cultural rules for when to talk and when to be silent, when and how to talk to others of different status or age, and when to be formal and when casual. But the home and playground may not be sufficient for all circumstances: different social settings can have different rules.

Schools are one setting with a special set of rules of use for academic language. It is richer grammatically (i.e., morphosyntactically), more varied in its style, and more well-formed and well-organized than casual home or playground language. Thus, children must be motivated to learn it too when they come to school. The more different academic language is from a child's home language, the more new rules of use the child will have to learn. Because Academic English is founded in middle- to upper-class language standards, students coming from a working-class or an immigrant community have an added burden in acquiring it, so the question of how to maintain motivation in demanding settings like schools becomes an issue.

The age of the student too may affect the difficulty of learning new rules of use. The younger child may have trouble discovering the differences between the old and new rules, whereas the older child may find it difficult to modify or inhibit old over-learned behaviors of use for new settings with more stringent or more sophisticated demands. For ELLs, how much schooling in their native language they may have had can also affect how well they adapt to the language standards of an American school. Some aspects, such as the need for well-formedness and rich vocabulary, may transfer well to the new setting whereas others, such as when and how to ask questions, may not. Thus, for any given child, the difficulty in learning to use Academic English may be compounded by multiple factors, making whatever natural motivation there is to participate in a new language community at school hard to sustain.

Cognitions too can guide language development. One view of the impetus for vocabulary acquisition is that children seek out words to express the ideas they have. Learning to express those cognitions (as well as new ones) in a new language is challenging, but, when they do so, children gain confidence that their past experiences are accessible and valued in a new setting. But children do not always develop a concept first and then search for a way to express it in language. As the spatial relations work cited above showed, even some fundamental concepts can be shaped by distinctions in a first language. Thus, how difficult or easy it is to translate cognitive understandings from one language to another depends on how different the concepts underlying the words in each of the languages may be. We will address this issue further in Chapter 3, when we discuss vocabulary and its relation to concepts.

Language and Education

Learning in school involves language. This truism encompasses the fact that traditional school learning cannot take place in the absence of language knowledge. A student must know how to read and write in the language of instruction. What we have tried to show in this chapter is that language, cognitive, and social skills are deeply and irrevocably intertwined. Indeed, language and language use is so pervasive and so important that literacy training cannot just be set apart from the rest of the curriculum. Literacy training in an ESL class is insufficient to give children the broad language skills they need to succeed. This is not to say that all language training should be integrated with other content classes. Research shows that separate instruction in English is valuable (August, et al., 2010). Rather, our argument is that it is not enough. The language used in content areas such as mathematics is different from the language typically used in other settings. For students to become literate in such areas, they must learn the specialized languages in the context of the content areas. Thus, all teachers need to understand both how language impacts learning in their discipline and the kinds of challenges children of diverse backgrounds may face when they have to comprehend and produce Academic English appropriate to a content area. This view of the inter-relations between language, cognitive, and social skills across all content areas holds several implications for educators.

1. Teachers need to motivate children to learn and use Academic English. Whatever the subject matter, and whatever the source of their language deficiencies, children need to become acquainted with the Academic English of each content area. Offering children the opportunity to translate what they know into whatever level of English they possess, and helping them express their experiences to others, conveys a sense of interest and value in their communications, thereby motivating more learning.

2. Children learn rules of use partly by observation as they acquire the language and partly by conversations about use. They cannot be expected to know how to use Academic English even if they have attended school elsewhere. Also, children who have not experienced much talk at home about others' thoughts and feelings, or who come from cultures where talking about others is less common, cannot be expected to have well-developed social behaviors that take account of others or follow US norms of interaction. Teachers need to know something about their students' cultural backgrounds. They need to model desired classroom behaviors and to talk about them and their role in learning in US schools.

3. Children's lexicons in their first language will influence their conceptual understandings even for some basic concepts. Thus, the notion that one can simply learn new vocabulary for old concepts is not completely correct. Sometimes the concepts underlying the words are not precisely alike, and word-for-word translations cannot be made. This fact complicates vocabulary learning, to say nothing of conceptual learning. Teachers need to be sensitive about the potential mismatch between underlying concepts in different languages and recognize why children may be reluctant just to do word-for-word translations when faced with vocabulary learning.

4. Children's language status, i.e., whether they have had exposure to more than one language, will affect much of their socio–cognitive behavior. Because the brain is so sensitive to language exposure early on, these changes are evinced even at young ages. All teachers need to know something about their students' language backgrounds, for example, when and how many languages they have been exposed to, as well as to understand how those experiences can benefit their cognitive and social capacities.

Summary

In this chapter we offered a view of language that is deeply connected to cognitive and social behaviors from infancy. We also presented a view of humans as social beings who come prepared to acquire language but who bootstrap those capacities by engaging others to help them learn more about their world. Language becomes both an object of learning and a tool for learning more. Within this framework, educators are like primary caregivers: they are charged with maintaining the motivation for learning and with providing the input for it, with patience and understanding of the process. In addition to bootstrapping, we introduced the complementary concept of scaffolding: teachers can best help their students to help themselves by providing a nearby platform for moving students' knowledge forward.

Unlike primary caregivers, teachers are presented with students who already have a range of experiences they bring to the school setting, and some of these may not provide an appropriate or adequate base on which to build toward the school's goals. Knowing how those backgrounds affect future learning, then, becomes an added responsibility for the teacher. What follows in Chapters 3 and 4 is what we think teachers need to know about languages and bilingualism to help them fulfill that responsibility.

Discussion Questions

- What is bootstrapping? What are the implications for classroom practice?
- How might cultural-language backgrounds influence the ways ELL students use language in the classroom?
- What do all teachers need to know about ELLs' first language and culture to teach ELLs effectively?
- How do ELL students' language and cultural backgrounds impact their mastery of the curriculum and engagement in all school activities?
- What is scaffolding, and why is teachers' use of it different from parents' use of it?

Chapter 3

How Languages are Alike and Different

Come let us go down, and there confound their language, so that they may not understand one another's language.

(Genesis 11: 1–9)

Why So Many Languages?

The question of why people speak so many different languages spawned one of the most well-known and revered Bible stories, that of the Tower of Babel. The story warns of the dire results when people aspire to be God-like and try to reach the heavens. What the tale does not reveal is that there are many ways to "confuse language" so that people cannot understand one another, from obvious ways to less obvious ones. Consider, for example, an obvious way: for every word in a language, a different word could be created in another language. If a group of people knew the words of only one of the languages, they would not be able to understand a speaker of the other language. But it would be relatively easy for them to dispel such a confusion. All they would have to do to learn the other language is to relate each word in their language with the corresponding word in the other language. Bothersome as that might be, it would not be so hard; it would be like learning that hot dog and frankfurter refer to the same thing and can be used in the same places in sentences. Unfortunately, although language "confusions" are common, word-for-word translations from one language to another almost never suffice to resolve them.

We are agnostic on the Tower of Babel story. We do not know for sure what an "original" language might have been like or whether there was ever only one. But we do know from studies of language history and language change that differences among languages crop up because languages continually change for many reasons, including movement of and interactions among peoples, regional differences in language use, and changes in social behavior. Confusions among languages can occur for these and other reasons on various levels. How we pronounce the words, how the words are constructed and put together to form sentences, and, importantly, how words relate to underlying concepts can all differ across languages. Add to these conditions the cultural differences in how and when language is used, and we see that learning and using a new language appropriately becomes a real challenge.

Nonetheless, there are more bilinguals than monolinguals in the world today. Clearly, learning another language is not impossible. That is because, although there are many differences across languages, there are similarities. Moreover, humans have remarkable faculties for acquiring languages. One of the similarities across languages is that they are all learnable by humans. However, just as circumstances of learning (such as exposure to language and opportunity to use it) can affect the quality of what infants acquire, so can relevant circumstances of learning affect the quality of second language acquisition. There is no single best accepted way to acquire a second language. What we do know is that circumstances of learning can vary greatly; ELLs' first language can affect the pattern of development as English is learned. Although teachers cannot possibly know all their students' first languages, they can develop an understanding of the kinds of differences among languages that may impact the kinds of errors they will see, and they can develop strategies to help students overcome them. In this chapter, we offer an overview of what teachers need to know to begin to appreciate what ELL students of different language backgrounds may face in acquiring English.

Components of Languages

Despite their specific differences, all human languages are systems that are composed of the same kinds of basic or general parts. The basic components of language are traditionally described as systems of phonology, semantics, and syntax—or, briefly, sound, meaning, and sentence structure. We prefer to think of the basic parts somewhat differently, as systems for expressing meanings through structured (e.g., governed by rules or accepted practices) articulation (e.g., modes of expression such as sound or sign).

The basic building blocks of languages include the smallest units that can carry meaning: phonemes (e.g., /p/, /b/) for distinctive sounds or articulations, and morphemes (e.g., *shoe, can, -s*) for distinctive meanings. For example, *bear* and *pear* are two different morphemes in English (*free* morphemes, or words). The *p* and *b* are the distinguishing phonemes. Adding a *bound* morpheme (e.g., *-s*) to a free morpheme (e.g., *bear*) results in a complex word (*bears*). There are also rules for combining words into sentences (syntax, e.g., rules that determine word order), and, finally, the conventions for use in various social contexts (*pragmatics* or language use, e.g., formal or informal uses such as *hello* versus *hi* or *cannot* versus *can't*).

Studying Language Similarities and Differences

Typology is the branch of language study dealing with similarities and differences across languages. The goal is to compare languages and classify them according to various characteristics in ways that reveal the range of human language types. Many characteristics of language have been considered.

However, the classificatory task has proven very difficult for several reasons. For one, the number of languages in the world is estimated to be between 4000 and 6000, and some are poorly documented; thus, any representative classification is a daunting task. For another, languages are notoriously inconsistent, with many exceptions, and it is difficult to make absolute or general claims about them. For a third, and importantly, the most readily observable characteristics of languages are usually superficial ones, and any one classification may reveal little of significance with regard to the range of types.

Traditionally, language typologists sought to describe languages in terms that would be compatible with any theory of language. However, it has become clear that many, if not all, formal terms for describing language have theoretical implications, having to do with underlying characteristics of human languages and their users' capacities. Consider, for example, the sentence, *The tall woman walks*. A *head* noun in language research is a central element in a noun phrase that governs (or influences) how the verb in such a sentence will be marked for agreement with it. Thus, *woman* is the head in the phrase *a tall woman* and governs the addition of the singular third person agreement marker *–s* on the verb *walk*. But researchers from different language theories do not always agree on what counts as a head. Hence, in recent years, efforts have been made to look for more abstract, within–theory patterns among languages as bases for grouping them. Those efforts have not yet resulted in fully accepted classifications. These problems suggest that, when we discuss similarities and differences among languages, we must recognize that the statements are more often relative than absolute; that is, they apply with high probability, but there are likely to be exceptions.

Language Universals

The ultimate similarity among languages is a statement about a universal property, a phenomenon that holds for each and every language of the world. Valid universals are hard to discover. Because not each and every one of the multitude of the world's languages can be examined, any candidate universal is necessarily based on only a sample of languages. It takes only one counter-example, a single language without that property, to prove that an "each and every" statement is not accurate.

Nonetheless, there are some universals that seem to stand the test of time. An example of a phonetic universal is that all verbal languages (i.e., not sign languages) have at least one sound that is a *stop*, i.e., the use of some place (e.g., tongue or lips) to impede the breath as it comes up the vocal tract. In English, *t* and *p* are examples of stops. However, languages do differ on where the stops are made and how many stop sounds they have. Thus, there are also statements called *implicational* universals, stated in if-then terms, which apply to only a subset of languages. An example is, "If a language has only one stop, it will be a *t*."

In addition to phonetic universals, there are universals among other components of language. For example, all languages make a distinction between entities and actions or states (e.g., nouns and verbs) among their parts of speech. So, all languages have parts of speech (or *lexical classes*), but languages differ with regard to what other classes they have (or even on what counts as a member of noun and verb classes). Also, some universals are *statistical*; they apply to most but not all languages. An example of a statistical universal about word order is, "In more than 90 percent of the world's languages, subjects (S) come before objects (O) in declarative sentences" (see Whaley, 1997).

Language Classifications

An alternative way of talking about similarities among languages is to say that they are in the same class. For example, one popular way of classifying languages describes them by their most common or basic word orders for subjects (S), verbs (V), and objects (O). Thus, SVO languages (English is one) are in a separate class from SOV languages like Japanese. However, these two common classes can be combined into one class depending on the criterion for classification. Languages with SOV and SVO orders are both in the class of S-before-O languages (along with the rarer category of VSO languages like Welsh) mentioned above as the statistical universal about word order. Thus, language universals can be about language classes.

Classification by language family has been another popular way of grouping languages that tend to share many characteristics, probably because of their evolutionary history. That is, they share a language ancestor and are often in geographical proximity. The sixteen major languages families are sub-dividable into families even more closely associated. Thus, Germanic languages like Dutch and German share more characteristics than Romance languages like Italian and Spanish, even though they are all Indo-European languages.

Importantly, being in the same family does not necessarily predict the particular features of a language's grammar. Here is an example using *subject dropping*, a language feature referring to whether a language can drop a subject from a sentence and still be considered well-formed. Chinese and Italian are from different language families but both can have well-formed sentences in which subjects are dropped, whereas Italian and French are from the same family but one can subject drop and the other cannot. For example, *piove* (__ *raining*) is grammatical in Italian, but, as in English, the *it* must be expressed overtly in French (*il pleut*). Therefore, whether two languages share a particular feature is not necessarily predictable from whether they share a familial status. Although there are family trees illustrating familial relationships, these are inadequate for predicting which particular grammatical features are shared.

Classifications based on grammatical characteristics have become popular in recent years, largely because discovering correlations among characteristics may help reveal something about the nature of human languages' allowable systems. For example, languages that allow subjects to be dropped have to have some way for listeners to determine what those subjects are. This can be accomplished, either through subject markings elsewhere in the sentence, as in Italian, which puts an ending on the verb to agree with the dropped subject, or through context (including prior discourse), as in Chinese. One might classify languages according to whether they mark the subject some way with a verb ending and then see whether they all allow subject dropping. If, like French, some do not, then there must be some other characteristic that blocks it. Such languages are considered like Italian at one level of the grammar (i.e., whether the verb is marked) but different on another (i.e., whether subject dropping is allowed). The search to discover the relevant determining characteristics of such languages can lead to rather abstract descriptions. However, by following such a program, researchers can make progress on how languages are alike and different in non–obvious ways.

Ideally, if all languages could be charted by grammatical characteristics on a single tree of language types, we could see where a particular language was on the tree and where it branched from other languages in terms of a host of different features. Figure 3.1 is a mini–instance of such a hierarchy. In that figure, languages divide into a tier of A languages (A) and B languages (B), depending on which of two values they have on a particular feature. In the following hypothetical example, we use the subject dropping feature we have already discussed to illustrate how the hierarchy works. Suppose A languages allow subject dropping and B languages do not allow it. Then, at the second tier, those two types divide according to values on some subordinate features. So, A languages might divide according to whether they mark the dropped subject on the verb (A1) or use discourse to identify the subject (A2). The third tier divides the languages again according to still other features. Now, say, A1 languages are divided into those that mark the subject on the main verb (A1a) and those that mark it on an auxiliary verb (A1b). B languages could be divided according to their own set of subordinate differences.

Unfortunately, we do not have such a single tree of language types. As of now, no language classifications result in perfect hierarchies of any appreciable size. There are so many different ways to divide languages across all their components that it is even difficult to imagine a single tree that would serve the purpose. Nonetheless, some kinds of less ambitious classifications are useful because each of them separates large numbers of languages into a relatively small number of language classes; and each class carries along with it a relatively large number of common characteristics, at least some of which are most probably due to common structural patterns and not to mere chance. Moreover, attempts at hierarchies can lead to new ways to describe similarities and differences.

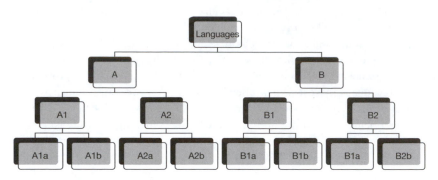

Figure 3.1 Ideal Language Hierarchy

Semantic and Pragmatic Variations

Language typologists have not ignored meaning but have chosen to focus primarily on variation across languages in how aspects of meaning are encoded in grammars of languages, for example, with case markings (in English, forms of personal pronouns such as *I-me* or *He-him*, the actor as *agent*, the affected one as *patient*), or tense (time) markings (in English, *will walk* for future, *walked* for past). It has more usually been anthropologists and psychologists specializing in language who have illuminated more directly the ways in which languages reflect how their speakers organize their worlds conceptually. For example, for labeling and categorizing objects, speakers of Yucatec Mayan depend more on the materials of which they are made than on their shape, whereas English speakers depend more on their shape (Lucy, 1992). Also, English marks all count nouns with plurals, some languages mark only the nouns for animates, and still others mark only the nouns for humans. Moreover, experiencing their native language is likely the way that young children learn what the important conceptual distinctions are for their culture. Research comparing English with languages as diverse as Korean and Spanish has shown that even young language learners are sensitive to how their first languages encode such basic concepts as space and agency. (See, for example, Bowerman & Choi, 2001; Martinez, 2000.)

Language communities also differ according to when and how language is used. The story of how Navaho children were initially disadvantaged in school settings because their culture encouraged silence among children is well known. Other differences may not be so familiar. For example, there is more than one way to learn how to become a knowledgeable, functioning member of a culture. In some cultures, children are encouraged to participate early and regularly, under adult guidance, in a community's everyday life. In contrast, European-American societies typically provide special settings for such learning away from everyday adult life (Rogoff, 1990). And, there are many ways in which language use can instantiate a community's values. In some cultures, children learn different ways of speaking for men and women, and in others there are specific forms of address for elders and conventions for how and when to speak to foreigners. For example, it is considered rude to make direct requests in Arabic of one's elders. Differences too can be found in whether languages mark the source of evidence for a statement, how a speaker signals belief or fact, and whether it is permissible to speak of others' internal states. All these sorts of devices and conventions influence the ways in which language learners will experience English and its use as alike or different from their home languages. Thus, learning a new language is not merely learning the grammar and vocabulary of another form of communication; learning how, where, and when to use the new language involves learning the ways in which one's language conveys an understanding of the social mores of the community.

Educational Implications

There are several ways the relationships among languages can influence the educational process. First, the kinds of errors an ELL makes in English may have to do with the nature of general differences between his or her home language and English. For example, languages are classified according to how much they rely on using free morphemes (e.g., words like *cat, the, run*) versus binding morphemes to a root (e.g., *re-* to roots like *do* or *use*). Expressing the relative time of an event can be done either way: we use a free morpheme to express the future (*will walk*) but a bound one to express the past (*walked*). Thus, a language like Vietnamese is classed as *isolating* because it rarely allows stringing together of morphemes to form a single word, but Turkish is classed as *agglutinative* because it regularly allows the binding of morphemes together into a single word. As our time example with *walk* shows, English falls somewhere in between (*will walk, walked*). If they transferred what they knew about their home languages, students from different home languages very well might produce differing patterns of English errors. A Vietnamese student might have trouble learning to attach plural morphemes when English allows it (e.g., "two shoe") whereas a Turkish home-language speaker might not. English marks what's called person agreement but only for third-person singular (e.g., *I sit, you sit, (s)he sits*). The Vietnamese student might have trouble adding that mark appropriately (e.g., "He sit"), whereas the Turkish student might overmark (e.g., "You sits"). Although the Vietnamese student makes two sorts of errors and the Turkish student only one, both patterns derive from the basic differences of their languages from English with regard to where they fall on the scale of how much languages combine morphemes into words. Teachers certainly cannot be expected to know how languages compare on this scale or other classificatory schemes, but they can be sensitive to the kinds of problems a student may have and can seek information and help in identifying underlying differences and difficulties, and how to overcome them. Also, the language charts in Chapter 6 illustrate many more examples of language differences that may have consequences for learning English.

Second, depending on the relations between English and the home language, as well as when they are exposed to English, students may have different strategies for learning English. Thus, with a home language that is very different in many ways from English, it may be easier to learn without much reference to the home language (I. Kovelman, personal communication), whereas one closely related to English might be easier to learn if more transfer is done. Interestingly, recent research suggests that many errors produced by ELLs can be traced to stages of language development rather than direct transfer from the home language (Paradis, 2007). This suggests that, indeed, when children are learning English, they may differ with regard to how much they rely on their home language, and even what they rely on it for. (See, for example, the section on consistency in Chapter 6.)

Also, recent research suggests earlier exposure to bilingualism is better than later, so, by the time they get to school, children exposed to both languages as infants may have a "bilingual" approach to languages that children exposed later do not. Findings like this are similar to those suggesting that young children are very flexible in their language learning, depending on their circumstances (both internal and environmental) and that there is more than one way to achieve the goal of overall language competence (Thomas & Karmiloff-Smith, 2005). Because this is a very new area of research, there is little that teachers can take from the current state of affairs other than to recognize that learning strategies may be different. They should be sensitive to the question of whether different strategies are being used by particular children and what those strategies might be.

Of course, teachers need to be sensitive as well to the myriad ways that English can differ from students' home languages, in terms not only of the various structural components of languages, but also their uses. We noted in Chapter 1 that Academic English, as the language of schooling, may be daunting even for students proficient in everyday English. Here we note that being proficient in everyday English as measured by tests of grammar and vocabulary may not capture what students know about conventional language use in the US, for example, in the workplace. Because everyday adult life may be very different from the home culture, students may be especially in need of guidance about the conventions of language use in the adult world.

Conclusion

Despite the many ways that languages can differ, there are several important similarities to keep in mind. All human languages have to be learnable, understandable, and capable of being produced by human users. They all have to do similar communicative work: users must be able to participate in their language community, to make assertions, ask questions, and make demands. Therefore all languages have to have ways to do these things. And, they are all subject to the changing, varied influences caused by use in real time and place. Because of this, languages are moving targets: language classifications are generally based on the typical or most frequently observed characteristics of a language at a point in historical time, and even the most regular and uniform language may have rare but acceptable alternatives. In one sense, any language user is a language learner. New words, expressions, and influences regularly impact our language, especially in the 21st century. Yet, languages are not as chaotic as they could be; they change, but not willy-nilly. They change slowly and in rather orderly ways. After all, they have to be somewhat orderly to be learnable and understandable.

Summary

As our range of examples shows, there are many ways to compare languages depending on how they typically or regularly accomplish communicative work. As examples, we offered comparisons on the basis of sounds (e.g., number of stops), constituent order (e.g., SVO, SOV), morpheme combining (e.g., isolating, agglutinative), subject–verb agreement (e.g., third person *s*), language–concept relations (e.g., object materials versus shapes), and language use (e.g., when to be silent and when to talk). For more on some of these as well as comparisons that we did not discuss, see Whaley, 1997.

We also described how language differences with English can impact students from different language backgrounds differently with regard to the kinds of errors they may make or what they find difficult. We suggested that students may choose different strategies for learning English, and that native bilinguals are very likely to be different from later second-language learners.

Finally, we proposed that the clue to understanding ELLs is to recognize how different learning English can be for them, depending on their first language and the circumstances of exposure and learning to both their first languages and to English. With a greater appreciation for the similarities and differences among languages, from sounds to language use, teachers may be better able to help individual students toward the road to successful English usage in all content areas. To assist teachers, we offer in Chapter 6 a series of charts that builds on the concepts in this chapter by providing gross comparisons between English and eight common languages found in US schools, organized around the characteristics that may be most influential in understanding where challenges to student success originate.

Discussion Questions

- In what ways can languages differ?
- What are some of the consequences of language differences for an ELL student's classroom performance?
- Why might ELL students differ in where they make errors in English?

- Is it good educational policy to treat ELLs as a homogeneous group? Why? Why not?
- What are the implications of all of the above for classroom practice, especially for optimally assisting ELL students in their learning?

Chapter 4

Becoming a Bilingual

Outside, Looking In

If you have ever been in a country in which your native language is not spoken, you may have found yourself at one time or another struggling to understand what was going on. You may have felt isolated from the life around you, and you may have realized how critical for social participation an understanding of the local language is. Even young children can have such experiences. Our anecdotes may seem familiar if you have traveled in a non-English speaking country; you may even have similar stories of your own. We offer these stories to illustrate how important language is, not only to social participation, but also to one's feelings of competence and self-worth.

1. We were in Tokyo trying to find the subway station near our hotel. Our ability to speak Japanese was virtually non-existent. When we tried to elicit aid from pedestrians on the street to ask directions, they turned away, refusing even to acknowledge our existence. "How rude" we thought, until a native later told us that it is considered shameful not to assist foreigners in need. The only way to avoid the shame is not to acknowledge the request, that is, pretend it did not occur. Apparently that is the reason we were ignored.

2. Returning from Italy where he had attended for six months a preschool in which no English was spoken, one of our children at age three entered an American preschool. A few months later, when an Asian child speaking no English joined his US class, he was the only child in the room who immediately engaged her, playing with her and "reading" books to her.

3. One of us recounted one day to a group of faculty wives a story about how helpless we had felt in Italy when, as we waited to get our visas, the conversation, in Italian with an Italian officer, turned to the issue of whether the US had the right to send nuclear warheads down major Italian highways. Our competence with the Italian language being limited to shopping in the market, I reported that we were way out of our depth on philosophical and political topics. A Japanese wife responded, "Now you know how it feels."

4. A native English speaker told us this story from her youth. Despite being well schooled in French, when she went off to France for a year of schooling, she found herself struggling to express her thoughts in class, and she began to doubt her own intellectual abilities. When she came back to school in the US and discovered she could readily add to classroom discussions, she said, "Oh, I'm smart after all!" She was so interested in her diverse experiences that she began to study linguistics, became an expert in languages and is now an honored professor at a major university.

Not knowing a community's language can be frustrating and even humiliating. Think, as that 3-year-old apparently did, what it must be like for young children who enter US classrooms with little or no understanding of English but who want to engage with others, or consider older ones who are supposed to master math, science, and social studies in a language not their own. Even children who know some English may feel like the professor did when confronted with sophisticated conversational topics—out of their depth on academic subjects. The first thing a teacher can do, then, for students of any age struggling with English, is to have empathy for their situation.

The issue of dealing with children inadequately skilled in the English language is not a new one for teachers; it has a history going back at least 100 years (Brisk, 2006). Nowadays, however, about 15 percent of students in US public schools have limited English proficiency (LEP). The number of different home languages and cultures that Dual Language Learners (DLLs) represent has grown: according to the 2000 US Census, there are more than 300 different languages spoken in US homes. In Chapter 3, we noted how many different ways languages can be alike and different and how these can impact learning English. The chapter ended with the argument that treating DLLs like a homogeneous group regardless of their language and cultural backgrounds for the purpose of achieving English proficiency was not good educational policy. A related (and still controversial) issue is what the educational goals should be for DLLs, as well as for the society as a whole. Should English proficiency be the only consideration, or should support for bilingualism be a goal as well? In the following sections, we report on recent research on bilingualism that educators need to be familiar with in order to have an informed answer to that question.

Acquiring English Proficiency

There is little argument that proficiency in English is necessary for academic success in US schools and that such success tends to have a positive impact on later life. There is disagreement, however, on how to achieve proficiency. On the one hand are those who believe the fastest way to English proficiency is total English immersion at the expense of home language development; on the other hand are those who believe that proficiency is best achieved when the home language is engaged in the service of learning, particularly of acquiring English proficiency. For this group, it is counter-productive to treat non-English speakers as if they have no worthwhile knowledge or background in language.

In Chapter 2, we argued that children use what they know to learn more. Because of this fact about how children develop, the only viable alternative, although to some extent the more demanding one for teachers, is to use what children already know (about their home language and culture) to learn about English and its use in school. For example, learning to read in the home language facilitates learning to read in English (Thomas & Collier, 1997). The question of how to assure English literacy for ELLs has a long history of controversy. Recent research comparing a transitional bilingual education program with a structured English immersion program over a five-year period found both to be roughly equally effective in the language and literacy outcomes produced by fourth grade (Slavin, *et al.*, 2011). For a variety of social, political, and economic reasons, full dual-language models have not become the norm in the US. However, there are many other possibilities for programs between the two extremes of total English immersion and full dual language. See Brisk (2010) for a discussion of some of them.

Because ELLs are not a homogeneous group with regard to language or cultural background, which native language children have been exposed to and how far along they are in acquiring it will impact how it can be used to assist in gaining English proficiency. Nonetheless, when home languages are not ignored but utilized in the learning of English, there can be more successful outcomes, not just for literacy but for other cognitive skills. This conclusion is based on a variety of ongoing research comparing children with experience in more than one language with monolinguals at all levels and ages, from infancy to school age, on measures from brain development to reading skills. In the remaining sections of this chapter, we describe some of that research to show that teachers can best serve their ELL students by recognizing and fostering their emergent bilingual status. In future chapters, we make practical suggestions for doing so.

Becoming Bilingual: Misconceptions and Advantages

It is important to note that, because of differences in their first language experiences, monolinguals can differ among themselves when they start to learn a second language. So, too, bilinguals are not a homogeneous group. Different amounts of knowledge and conditions of acquisition for the second language also distinguish individuals who have had at least some experience in more than one language. Historically, a distinction was made between those with equivalent skills in two languages and those with dominance in one language over another. A recent, related metric is level of proficiency attained in the languages. Of course, dominance and levels of proficiency can change over time. A more stable distinction is that between those learning two languages simultaneously in infancy and those doing so sequentially later in childhood. Recent research has shown important differences among such types, even at the level of brain activity.

Comparing bilinguals and monolinguals, then, must be done cautiously, with these distinctions in mind. Although bilinguals are a varied group, it is important to think of them as different from monolinguals: generally they are not just like monolinguals except for having two languages instead of one in their brains. Researchers are investigating just how different bilingual brains are, but already we know that children exposed to more than one language can be different in many ways, depending on the type and timing of their exposure. Some of these differences may facilitate learning, while others may not, but teachers need to know what the differences are and how to make use of them to maximize bilinguals' learning. Moreover, some ELLs are monolinguals when they start to learn English, whereas some are DLLs and may have enough skills in multiple languages to be considered bilingual as they progress in English. There is no precise definition of the level of proficiency needed in each language to be called "bilingual."

What We Know Now: Misconceptions

Processing Speed

The nature and course of speech processing development in infancy is influenced by exposure to the languages heard. (See Conboy, 2010; Polka, Rvachew, & Mattock, 2007, for reviews.) All infants in the first year or two of life are busy acquiring the sound systems (phonology) of the languages they hear. They start out being sensitive to all contrasts utilized by languages and gradually learn to focus on the distinctions in their surrounding community of speakers while gating out, or ignoring, the others. Infants hearing more than one language tend to keep the "gate" open a bit longer than infants hearing only one; hence, they may show less proficiency in identifying sounds of the language heard by both sorts of infants but are more able to notice relevant contrasts in another language than those with exposure to only one. Moreover, at just a few months of age, infants regularly exposed to more than one language can distinguish the languages they have heard. Children exposed to two languages early are better able to distinguish those languages' sounds than children learning a second language later. We do not yet know how much exposure is necessary for early optimal sound system discriminations. We do know that relearning to distinguish previously ignored sounds is possible; however, it may take many hours of concentrated practice for adults to recover lost contrasts, such as the distinction between r and l for Japanese and Korean speakers. Many aspects of the accents of non-native speakers of English are due to the fact that recovering gated-out contrastive sounds can be difficult. (See Best, 1994, on recovery of lost contrasts.)

Not surprisingly, the brain's responses to hearing words are also influenced by exposure to more than one language. Regardless of their vocabulary size, monolingual toddlers show large and rapid responses to known versus unknown words; bilingual children show similar patterns for their dominant language, but only those with large vocabularies do so for the non-dominant language as well. The importance of vocabulary size suggests that experience with a language's cues to word recognition speeds processing. For example, stress patterns, initial consonants, and vowel information are cues to a word, but the usefulness of these cues can vary among languages. Children learning two languages may need more information to resolve conflicting cues and may be unable to do so quickly. Moreover, depending on their stage of learning, they may not even be able to access the relevant cues. Such differences between monolinguals and bilinguals on speed of processing might be interpreted as general language impairment when in reality they are likely due to the need for more time and experience in dealing with more complex language exposure.

Code Switching

Moving between two languages—sometimes in the same sentence—is common among adult bilinguals; although its nature varies with situation and languages, where and how it occurs is not random but is rule-governed. Young children in bilingual home environments typically experience code switching and begin to use it themselves at an early age. Early views of code switching were negative: children were said to fall back on their first language when they lacked a word in their second. Instead, recent study shows that code switching can do much more than merely filling lexical gaps. It can serve many purposes, drawing on sophisticated knowledge of languages and their usages. Although the uses and types of code switching change with development, by preschool age, children are able to handle it quite well, typically following the lead of the adults in their environment with regard to its kinds and uses. (See Reyes & Ervin-Tripp, 2010.)

However, speed of processing is also affected by code switching: recent research shows that switching between words in two languages slows processing compared with presentations of words in each language separately (Conboy, 2010). This is more evidence that a bilingual's possible "slowness" with language may be a symptom of dual language processing rather than general language impairment. (See Chapter 8 for more on distinguishing English-learning problems for genuine general language impairment.)

Vocabulary

Similarly, small vocabulary size in itself is not a sufficient indicator of general language impairment. Although bilingual vocabulary size in a single language has often been reported to be less than that of monolinguals, the disparity tends to disappear when the combined vocabulary size across bilinguals' languages is compared with monolinguals' (Pearson, Fernandez, & Oller 1993). Nonetheless, it is important to note that bilinguals do not necessarily have translation equivalents (i.e., two words for one underlying concept) for the words in their respective language lexicons. Rather, they often have unique word–concept pairs in each language. There is a good conceptual reason for this: the concept underlying a word in a language may not be identical to the concept underlying the "equivalent" word in the other language. For example, Japanese has one word for swallowing non-solid entities such as smoke and water. There is no such word in English; the word *drink* is not appropriate to smoke. So, bilingual children may be appropriately cautious learners when it comes to taking up apparent translation equivalents. Moreover, if they already have a word for an object, they may be cautious about acquiring another one in violation of the principle of *mutual exclusivity*, which states that, all other things being equal, learners should assume one name for one object (Markman, 1991). Again, we should be cautious about judging bilinguals as generally language impaired because they seem to have small vocabularies in one language. To use words appropriately, bilingual children need to learn any subtle differences in the languages' word–concept relations.

How can educators help children overcome the conceptual-lexical problem? One way is to take advantage of the fact that DLLs are aware of the existence of different languages very early, even before they understand much else. For example, a 2-year-old learning both English and Greek was visiting a farm in the US, and asked her mother, "This cow speaks English, right, Mommy?" However, understanding what goes into the concept underlying the word is not typically a subject in awareness. Teachers need to make it so. Even in pre-school, discussions about words and how their meanings may be alike and different in two languages help children see how words and concepts relate across languages. Later chapters present more on word relationships and how to foster such discussions in classes.

What We Now Know: Advantages

Thus far, we have discussed ways in which becoming bilingual may change the tempo of the acquisition process and result in performance indicators that can be misinterpreted as general language impairment. Instead, we have argued these can be consequences of the need for processing more language material. Now we turn to two aspects of behavior for which recent findings have supported advantages for bilinguals over monolinguals: *understanding of mental state* and *executive function*. Many questions remain to be answered, especially with regard to the robustness of the findings. Will they apply to all bilinguals, regardless of their conditions of learning or level of proficiency? Are they long-lasting and do they apply in a broad array of circumstances? Although we do not yet have all the answers to such questions, the findings are sound; they are based on multiple studies with many participants. While future research will clarify their scope, the basic conclusions are not likely to be overturned.

Understanding of Mental State

The ability to take a perspective other than one's own is a cornerstone of socio-cognitive thinking and reasoning. All tasks used to study mental state understanding require children to exercise a kind of cognitive control by suppressing their own perspective or knowledge in order to focus on the mental state of another. Research into mental state understandings (theory of mind, TOM, is a common descriptive term) showed that preschoolers under the age of four were unable to set their own reality aside to describe accurately the false beliefs of others (Wimmer & Perner, 1983). The false belief tasks involved a child witnessing the substitution or movement of an object previously seen by an observer who did not see the later transformations. The child was then asked whether the observer now knew what the new object was or what the new location of the original object was. Not all aspects of mental state understanding have yet been studied. Nonetheless, recent work has clarified the early findings by showing that younger children can pass less demanding tasks involving false belief; it has also addressed how language status may affect understanding of mind. For example, one question was whether monolingual children who speak a language like Turkish, which has specific words (*san, zannet*) meaning "believes falsely," perform better on such tasks than children who speak languages like English that has no specific false belief words. (The test did not use specific false belief terms, but asked what the observer would "look for" or where the observer would "look.") Although language had some influence, the economic status of families mattered more than the particular language spoken (Shatz, *et al.*, 2003).

However, research has shown that merely being bilingual does have an impact on understanding of mind. Bilinguals generally perform better than monolinguals on TOM tasks. (See Siegal, *et al.*, 2011, for a review.) Bilingual children of different ages speaking a variety of languages exhibit the effect at least some of the time. The ability of very young bilinguals to adjust their speech is limited by their language resources and by contextual demands, but even 2-year-olds are sensitive to language differences in their interlocutors. Chinese monolingual preschoolers whose language, like Turkish, has specific false belief terms do less well on TOM tasks than Chinese–English bilinguals (Goetz, 2003). So, bilinguals have an advantage over monolinguals on understanding of mental state, even when compared with monolinguals with a language having specific false belief terms. For quite a while researchers believed that this bilingual advantage on TOM tasks was based on essential experience in conversational interactions involving only one language, thereby requiring the bilingual child to inhibit the other language. That is, having conversational experience in using each of two languages would be required before any advantages in inhibitory ability in other domains like understanding of mind would be achieved.

Does inhibitory ability originate in conversational experience or does it have earlier roots? Recent research offers an answer. All infants come biologically prepared to attend to and process information in their environments. However, 7-month-old infants exposed to more than one language are better at attending to one visual signal over another than are infants exposed to only one language (Kovacs & Mehler, 2009). That is, even at pre-linguistic ages, infants already differ as a result of their experience processing varied language input: as a group, infants with bilingual exposure exhibit better cognitive control of inhibitory and attention processes, and this may have implications for advantages in later behaviors like mental state understanding. While more research is needed to cement such ties, our point is that the influence of bilingual experience can begin very young and have very far-reaching consequences. Conversations may be where bilingual children practice cognitive control with language and where cognitive control manifests itself most readily in bilingual preschoolers, but cognitive control can be observed even before children use language in conversations. Nonetheless, language exposure may be especially well suited to facilitate infant learning of cognitive control because infants are well prepared to attend to language. We do not know whether infants can learn to manage attention as well in cognitive conflict situations involving non-language stimuli.

Executive Function

Building on the notion of cognitive control, the construct of executive function (EF) is broader than it; EF is clearly important to education. EF refers to a collection of brain processes that are implicated in all higher-level cognitive activity such as self-regulation and abstract thinking. Developing over time in children, EF appears to influence ability to direct attention, control inhibition, manage working memory, and switch between alternatives. Tasks measuring EF examine the construct's sub-components with, for example, tests of resolution of conflicting information, delay of gratification, working memory (digit span), and direction of attention (Attention Network Task). There is at present no precise definition of EF or exact specification of the range of tests to be used to assess it. Because bilinguals have practice alternating between their two languages (in either comprehension or production), their experience may reasonably be expected to facilitate the development of at least some aspects of EF.

Since 1999, when Bialystok proposed that bilinguals might outperform monolinguals on executive function tasks, she and others have been investigating which of the composite skills labeled by EF show a bilingual advantage. (See, for example, Bialystok, 1999; 2011.) Although more research is needed to study all the components, already researchers have demonstrated that bilingual children often outperform their monolingual peers on EF tasks, especially those that involve resolving some sort of competing demands, such as directing attention to one of two attractive stimuli or inhibiting one's own perspective when trying to take account of another's. The bilingual advantage is robust: it has been observed among speakers of multiple languages and in comparisons of cultures with different social values. However, as with TOM studies, task type and testing conditions influence findings: for children up to kindergarten age, the bilingual advantage is typically limited to tests involving conflict resolution; older bilinguals (age six and over) doing complex working memory tasks also show an advantage there, whereas younger ones doing simpler (but supposedly age-appropriate) working memory tasks do not. Thus, how general the bilingual advantage is across putative EF tasks is not clear.

An important caution on the bilingual–monolingual comparison research has to do with socio-economic status (SES) of study participants. Most studies simply equate groups for SES; there is very little work on differences among SES classes. The few research reports on young children confirm a robust bilingualism advantage: even bilingual children from lower SES groups do better directing attention in conflicting situations than do monolinguals. However, the question of whether the bilingual advantage is maintained throughout the school years and beyond is a controversial one. Work to date suggests that the advantage may wax and wane throughout the lifespan, as children acquire new skills during the school years, as young adults reach the apex of their lifetime processing abilities, and as memory and processing skills wane with age.

Language Registers

Registers refer to various styles of language use that describe how language is used with different interlocutors in different contexts. For example, the register, or style of language, a mother would use with a young child differs from one she would use with friends at a book club meeting or out to dinner. Registers allow for recognition of differences or similarities in age, gender, power, status, and knowledge between conversational participants. They draw on vocabulary (including jargon and idioms), grammar, and pronunciation to establish social relations such as formality and solidarity between speakers.

All language users, including monolinguals, have a variety of within-language registers at their command. Even 4-year-olds speak differently from 2-year-olds and to parents or peers (Shatz & Gelman, 1977). However, bilinguals can also use their languages as registers, for example, speaking their home language in order to exclude from the conversation those who don't understand it. Anthropologists have reported on multilingual teens who use different aspects of their languages to reflect solidarity with immigrants from the same locale or to signal their membership in a particular community (e.g., Bailey, 2000). Code switching with other code switchers but not with monolinguals is another example of bilinguals' facility with registers. Because they are familiar with different ways of speaking in different contexts, it may help DLLs to see that Academic English is a kind of formal register appropriate to educational settings.

Summary: What Have We Learned?

1. We cannot ignore children's previous language and cultural experience. The challenge is how to recognize where it might help and where it might delay in acclimating an ELL to the American school environment and the use of English.
2. ELLs are a varied group, not only due to age and experience but also to language and cultural differences.
3. The brain reflects exposure to more than one language, and differences can be observed at very young ages. Multi-language exposure can have broad influences beyond language.
4. Processing of language material may take longer in ELLs but should not be mistaken for general language impairment.
5. Code switching is a skill that develops with experience and is not a sign of deficit.
6. Concepts underlying language expressions can vary; translation equivalents are rare. This makes learning vocabulary in a second language harder than one might think.
7. Bilingualism facilitates understanding of mind and executive function, at least in children in the early grades. Whether and how that advantage is maintained over time is unclear.
8. Bilinguals have early experience and some facility with language registers in social settings. This may help generate understanding about Academic English.

Discussion Questions

*   What are some of the differences in bilinguals and what are their consequences?
*   Is there such a thing as direct or exact translation? Why? Why not?
*   Is speed of processing language a good metric on which to judge the intelligence of ELLs? Why? Why not?
*   What is executive function and how might it be facilitated by knowing more than one language?
*   What is code switching and how is it a benefit or burden for ELLs?
*   How does dual language learning affect cognitive development, and what is the role of direct instruction by classroom teachers in this process?

Part II

How to Teach English Language Learners

In Part II, we discuss the use of checklists and rating scales, language comparison charts, and grade-appropriate suggestions for including language learning in lessons. All of our proposals are designed to help teachers manage the task of making their instructional plans most responsive to the particular needs of the varied students, including English language learners, in their classrooms.

Chapter 5

Help Yourself and Get Help!

Help Yourself with Checklists and Rating Scales

All humans are subject to errors, lapses in memory, and disorganization. A recent book on hospitals recounts how simple modifications in practice (in this case, the use of what we call *minder checklists*) can result in better outcomes (Provonost & Vohr, 2010). In that spirit, we offer three tools, *minder checklists* and two observational tools, *observer checklists and rating scales*, which can help teachers organize and facilitate students' learning in classrooms. We offer them as methods to help teachers organize and keep track of the language backgrounds of the students in their classrooms, to help monitor their own communication with students and their parents, and to track the strategies they use to facilitate learning, including the progress of English Language Learners (ELLs).

Minder Checklists

Minder checklists organize information teachers need to know and then help maintain it in awareness. If such checklists are filled out early in the school year and kept handy for reference throughout the year, they will help maintain attention to ongoing concerns and needs. An example of a minder checklist, one that a teacher can fill out after getting the relevant information from her students, is the language "map" of students in the classroom in Table 5.1. There a teacher can list for each student, for example, whether the student is an English speaker, what the home language is, what English speakers there are in the household, and the years of ELL instruction a student may have had. The teacher can add or subtract from the headings as appropriate.

A second example in Table 5.2 is a self-assessment checklist teachers can use to keep track of their behaviors mandated by a particular instructional approach; this can be used to record both oral and written language. A third example is the minder checklist for sources of help (see Table 5.3) assisting teachers in keeping track of whether and when they have utilized the sources for help discussed later in this chapter. Minder checklists tend to be simple:

teachers can fill them out themselves, modify the forms as needed for their own purposes, and add new information (e.g., a new ELL student or a new help source) throughout the year. The Sheltered Instruction Observation Protocol—SIOP (Echevarria, Vogt, & Short, 2000) is one example of a commonly used observation protocol yielding potentially useful results for teachers. Additionally, in Chapter 7, we provide another example of a teacher behavior checklist (Table 7.4), which can be used to record either or both oral and written language. Readers should feel free to copy the checklists in this volume and use them for their own purposes.

Observational Checklists and Rating Scales

We believe that direct observation in the classroom is a key to understanding what is happening with all students—particularly those who struggle academically as they simultaneously learn Academic English as the language of schooling. Observation is more than looking at classroom activity. It is a method of inquiry about students, the instructional practices in which they participate, the classrooms in which they learn, and the social situations within which teaching and learning take place (Silliman & Wilkinson, 1991). Careful observations can capture and clarify the school realities with which students struggle. These descriptions, in turn, can serve as the basis for teachers to make informed judgments about 1) students' progress as they develop needed skills across the curriculum and 2) teachers' instructional effectiveness in promoting that development. Direct observation is a method for revealing ELLs' knowledge and their use of key skills.

Observational checklists and rating scales are two observational tools providing systematic examination of students' or teachers' language use in the classroom. Both tools have the same aim: to create an accurate written record of how students and/or teachers use language so that teachers have a solid basis for conclusions on which to build plans supporting student progress. Although the tools are somewhat different, they both have to address common factors. Whether creating or using either a checklist or rating scale, one needs to be sure to attend to each of these factors:

- Observational Focus: Who do you look at or listen to (e.g., student, teacher, both)?
- Content Focus: What do you want to learn about and focus on (e.g., oral language use)? Assisted (as a response) or unassisted (spontaneous)?
- Coding Unit: What are the relevant behaviors to count (e.g., oral requests for information, written sentence production)?
- Collecting Information: How will you record data (checklist, rating scale, both)?
- Setting: Where do you want to collect the information (e.g., in response to teacher-led whole-group lessons, in small groups, students pairs)?

- Purpose: Why are you collecting this information (e.g., to evaluate a student's achievement, progress, strengths, weaknesses)? (Silliman & Wilkinson, 1991).

An account of a particular child's specific behaviors (e.g., amount and type of oral language participation) that calls for direct observation over a period of time may require an additional observer to record the data. An aide, student teacher, or parent might be recruited for this job. Typically, such observers do not participate in the activity under observation, but they must be instructed carefully on what to do before the observation. There is no time for learning on the spot, since decisions about what to check off on the worksheet/form need to be made with split-second timing during the observation (Silliman & Wilkinson, 1991). Observers should also discuss their record with the teacher, to arrive at agreement.

Whoever is doing the coding and whatever particular checklist or rating scale is used, there is a tendency to embellish or see things from one's own perspective and to fill in details that may not be there. It is important to try to observe from the viewpoint of the individual being observed, to make clear distinctions between what has been seen or heard and the conclusions to be drawn, and not to draw any unwarranted conclusions (Irwin & Bushnell, 1980).

All the tools we discuss here are based on pre-determined categories. That is, answers to the questions such as those asked above about what will be recorded (content focus) and how (collecting information) are determined beforehand. These categories should be based on what teachers have found to be important from their own experience or from prior research. We do not advocate using observational tools in a more descriptive or narrative way to develop the categories themselves; such work, while often done by researchers, is resource-heavy and requires considerable time and training (Silliman & Wilkinson, 1991).

However, the level of detail in categories can vary, depending on a teacher's goals and the resources available. For example, Table 5.4 displays a checklist for determining whether an ELL uses oral language in class. A teacher may want to modify the content focus of the 5.4 checklist to learn more about the way the student participates, and, for some purposes such as that, situational differences may seem less important. So, instead of separating formal and informal situations, the checklist in Table 5.5 asks how the child participates, *offering comments, answering questions,* and *asking questions.* Again, teachers could modify these checklists to suit their own topics and purposes.

Checklists can vary in how data are recorded. For some categories and purposes, information may simply be coded as *yes* or *no,* or with a checkmark. Some categories benefit from quantitative descriptions. The checklists in Tables 5.4 and 5.5 could be coded with *yes/no* or an observer could count the times a child participates by placing a mark in the appropriate column for each child behavior. When the marks are all tallied, the teacher has a record of the

Table 5.1 Classroom Language Map

Name	Age	Native English speaker?	Other language(s) spoken	English speaker at home?	Age of exposure to English	Identified as ELL?	Years receiving services	Literate in English?	Literate in home language?

Table 5.1 continued

Summary	Numbers	Language preference
Students		
Native English speakers		
Bilinguals		
Identified ELLs		

Teacher name: _____

Date of observation: _____

Situation/activity: _____

Table 5.2 Teachers' Checklist for Instructional Modifications

Uses sheltered language forms of English	
Uses culturally relevant resources and activities to teach basic content	
Uses scaffolding sequences in instruction	
Uses a diverse set of questions	
Emphasizes developing language skills through content lessons	
Recasts student responses with appropriate content and English language forms	
Uses visual support, including gestures, to reinforce meaning	
Models the steps needed to complete lessons	
Emphasizes comprehension throughout lessons	
Avoids over-correcting students' errors in grammar and pronunciation	
Emphasizes global aspects of concepts and shows connections to curriculum overall	

Teacher name: _____

Date of observation: _____

Situation/activity: _____

Source: Adapted from Becker, A. & Parker, R. (2010) Project BRITE Professional Development Workshop. Providence, RI: The Education Alliance at Brown University, June 18, 2010.

Table 5.3 Sources of Help

Sources	Name	Contact	Date	Follow-up school	Follow-up home
School					
ESL teacher					
Bilingual teacher					
Bilingual aide					
Speech-language pathologist					
Others					
Home					
Parents					
Relatives					
Friends					
Beyond					
Local college/ university					
Refugee center					
Public library					
School district					
Others					
Printed sources (Appendix)					
Web sources (Appendix)					

Table 5.4 Checklist for Student's Oral Language

	Informal situations	*Formal situations*
Does the student participate orally?		
Does the student appear to listen attentively to peers?		
Are the student's oral contributions relevant/responsive to the topic?		
Does the student speak audibly?		
Does the student use standard English?		
Does the student use L1 or code switch?		
Does the student change oral language style in different situations?		

Student: _____

Date of observation: _____

Situation/activity: _____

Source: Adapted from Genishi, C. & Dyson, D. (1984) *Language assessment in the early years* (p. 204). Norwood: Ablex Publishing Corporation.

Table 5.5 Expanded Checklist for Student's Oral Language

Student's language	
Participates orally	
Asks/answers questions	
Asks clarification questions	
Commands	
Explains	
Persuades	
Describes action/object/event	
Listens attentively to peers/teacher(s)	
Provides relevant/responsive topical contributions	
Initiates a topic	
Elaborates a topic	
Maintains a topic	
Initiates a topic shift	
Speaks audibly	
Speaks using Standard English	
Code switches	
Changes oral language according to situations	
Role play	
Instruction	

Teacher name: _____

Date of observation: _____

Situation/activity: _____

Table 5.6 Rating Scale for Student's Oral Language

	Often	*Rarely*	*Never*
Does the student participate orally?			
Does the student appear to listen attentively to peers and teachers?			
Are the student's oral contributions topically-relevant?			
Are the student's oral contributions topically-responsive?			
Does the student use Standard English?			
Does the student code switch to L1?			
Does the student change oral language style in different situations?			

Student: _____

Date of observation: _____

Situation/activity: _____

Source: Adapted from Genishi, C. & Dyson, D. (1984). *Language assessment in the early years* (p. 204). Norwood: Ablex Publishing Corporation.

frequency of the behaviors in the time the child was observed. The duration an observation period lasted should always be recorded.

Checklists can be modified to serve as rating scales by using frequency ratings such as *often*, *rarely*, and *never*. To create such a rating scale, if there are resources and time, the ratings could be based on the observational checklist made earlier; that is, teachers could decide to categorize some range of behaviors marked on a 5.4- or 5.5-type checklist as *often* or some smaller range as *rarely*. Such ranges would reflect what they observed more generally across students in the classroom (e.g., three or more questions for a student might be considered *often*, one or two *rare*). Alternatively, teachers with few additional resources such as other observers may simply want to fill out a rating scale based on her impressions of each student. They can then check those impressions with their own close observations of their students to be sure they have made accurate determinations of the students' participation. Although this is not the preferable approach, it does take into account limited resources. However, because this latter way may be less objective than the former one, teachers using it should periodically check on the reliability of their earlier impressions. In either case, teachers should note on their written records which approach they are using.

Table 5.6 illustrates how the checklist in Table 5.4 has been modified to be a rating scale.

Tools such as these can be used to track a student's progress by comparing observations done later in the year with the earlier records. Also, the written forms make a useful record to share with a student's other teachers, including English as a Second Language (ESL) teachers.

Differences between Observational Checklists and Rating Scales

Observational checklists are a practical means to document on the spot a student's oral language use in a particular activity. With them one can obtain a relatively large amount of information that can be represented in numerical form. Questions such as the following can be addressed using checklists: "How often does the student ask questions during a classroom lesson?" In contrast, rating scales are typically used at the end of an observation period to sum up the cumulative effect of a period of direct observations. They are more often used to assess global constructs such as overall question asking, talkativeness in English, or print awareness. Rating scales typically entail more evaluation than observational checklists in that the codings themselves are ranked relative to one another (e.g., *often–rarely*, *frequent–infrequent*). Hence, the codes can involve more implied or stated qualitative judgments about the behaviors.

Advantages and Disadvantages of Checklists and Rating Scales

A major advantage of checklists and rating scales is that they can be a practical means to document students' oral language use in particular activities. The tools are relatively easy to use, including tallying results after observations, and interpretation can take relatively little time as well. Moreover, a comparatively wide range of behaviors can be observed during one session.

However, these tools do take some effort to develop and/or modify. Because the decisions about which behaviors to focus on must be made prior to observation, the tools have to be carefully developed/chosen, and the individuals who will use them must learn how to use them and be comfortable about making on-the-spot decisions with them. Unless the observer is very comfortable in using the tools, the information recorded will not be reliable and thus not useful. For example, if the intent is to classify the types of questions that an ELL voluntarily answers, the observer must be familiar with the various types of questions (e.g., *wh-*, *yes/no*, *clarification*, etc.). Rating scales have been found to be most prone to error for the untrained (Irwin & Bushnell, 1980). Box 5.1 presents the most common types of errors in using rating scales.

Another disadvantage is that, although summarizing the information collected is not difficult, interpreting the information may be a bit more of a challenge. This is because of the lack of information about contextual details or behaviors such as intonation and gestures accompanying the language. Also, deciding on the duration of the observation can be arbitrary and therefore the data may not fully capture what students know or can do with English in the classroom. At best, by themselves the records are a snapshot; they are not a compendium of a student's complete communicative repertoire (Rymes, 2010).

Hints for Creating Forms for Observational Tools

Make the observation forms in advance and include essential features—the name of the student(s) to be observed, date of observation, and contextual features such as situation, activity, and time of day and length of observation. These will be significant for interpreting the information at a later time. The body of the form then lists the categories to be coded and spaces to code or rate. (See the previous tables in this chapter for examples of successful forms.) As discussed above, list the specific behaviors of interest separately on the form rather than using a more overarching category (compare Tables 5.4 and 5.5). Organize the list logically so that it is easy to use. Behaviors expected to be frequent should be listed near the top of the page while infrequent behaviors should be listed near the bottom. Organize the list to be consistent with the stated purpose of the observation. If the interest is a particular student's oral language during a small workgroup activity, then there should be a worksheet just for that student in that activity. One cannot assume, for example, that if there are six students

---

Box 5.1 Common Errors in the Use of Rating Scales

- **Error of leniency**: Raters tend to rate those they know higher than they should be rated, or, to compensate for possible error, raters rate them lower than they should be rated.

- **Error of central tendency**: Raters avoid extremes of high or low in their ratings and rate toward the middle.

- **"The halo effect"**: Raters often do allow some irrelevant information to influence ratings, which confuses the ratings.

- **Error of logic**: Raters often give similar ratings for two aspects that seem logically related.

- **Error of contrast**: Raters either tend to rate people in the opposite direction from themselves or rate them as similar to themselves, depending on how they are perceived and how the aspect is rated.

- **Proximity error**: Raters often evaluate aspects next/close to each other in time or space in a more similar way than items with greater separations.

Source: Adapted from Irwin, D. & Bushnell, D. (1980). *Observational strategies for child study* (pp. 213–214). New York: Holt.

---

in the group an accurate description of what a particular student says during the activity can be arrived at by dividing total oral language recorded on the list by six. (See Irwin & Bushnell, 1980, for more on constructing robust observational forms.)

We would add that these observational tools are only helpful if they are used and used accurately. Therefore, it is best to keep them as simple as possible. It may be better to create more than one form rather than to cram everything you want to know onto one. For example, you could record a student's oral participation on one form but address the student's use of non-standard forms on another.

Conclusion

Observational checklists and rating scales are characterized by having pre-determined categories; they allow for observation and recording of a wide range of language behavior over time and across settings for either students or teachers or both. By and large, they are relatively inexpensive (in time and money) and efficient to use. They are essentially classification systems that are used as events unfold (checklists) or at the end of a period of observation (rating scales). Checklists are more commonly used for tracking progress than are rating scales. Summarizing the information collected is not difficult. Interpreting the information, however, may be a bit more of a challenge because of the absence of detailed contextual information and specific information about the quality of the behavior observed (e.g., intonation and gestural cues). Checklists and rating scales are best used to get an overall sense of an English language learner or his or her teacher's use of language in school situations. They should be not be used, however, for the complete evaluation of a student struggling with learning English.

Get Help: "It Takes a Village . . ."

We paraphrase the by-now famous book title about needing a village to raise a child (Clinton, 1996): we believe that it takes a community of educators, parents, and concerned individuals to help ELLs become successful students in US schools. Thus, to further facilitate teachers' efforts in educating ELLs, we suggest that they get help as a regular part of their work with them. We offer two kinds of suggestions: The first is for teachers to embrace teamwork and cross-disciplinary collaboration among all of the educational staff serving ELL students. The second suggestion is to actively pursue resources on the web, at local community integration centers, and within the districts themselves.

Regarding the first suggestion, collaboration is the key. Interaction, coopera-tion, and assistance among specialists and classroom teachers are essential for the school success of all students (Bailey, 2010). Each educational professional with the school brings a point of view for inquiry and instruction/intervention. The issues facing educators and specialists in today's school include 1) keeping up with the demands of a challenging and changing curriculum; 2) meeting the specific needs of students who are challenged to keep up, such as ELL students; and finally, 3) understanding what the student is going through, particularly when several professional educators provide complementary and in some cases overlapping services for the same students. Members of different disciplines, all with well-meaning instructional and interventional goals, are challenged themselves to develop and implement collaboratively related programs that will maximize students' language and literacy learning. The question is, however, "What language abilities are required or assumed to underlie the various academic tasks facing ELL students on a daily basis?" Once that question is addressed, then the issue becomes how educational professionals can work together so that they complement and not replicate one another. Often this does not happen naturally. Teachers must help to create a school community where there are both time and opportunities for regular classroom teachers to collaborate with specialists. In so doing, all specialists—speech-language pathologists, read-ing specialists, ESL teachers—can join with content teachers to co-create teaching strategies, review the progress of ELLs in their classes, and identify key resources that can be applied to the education of ELLs. Such efforts, especially in the context of collaborative team activities, deserve everyone's support.

A further activity of such collaborations should be to extend beyond the boundaries of the school proper and find ways to bridge the gap between school and home with regard to language and literacy practices. Support for home visits and preparing to speak with parents respectfully, without jargon, are two suggestions for encouraging more home–school communication. Arranging for family members to visit the classroom, possibly to talk about their homelands or to help with projects related to ethnic or national identity, is another.

Regarding the second suggestion, we encourage teachers to actively pursue resources beyond home and school. Community and district facilities such as local refugee centers, community colleges, and university international student centers offer opportunities to find translation and communication assistance for teachers and parents. Local libraries, as well as schools of education, may offer resources such as materials or an expert speaker series. The internet provides a wealth of useful information. The reader should consult Appendix A for a list of useful web resources.

Summary

We proposed two different kinds of tools, 1) minder checklists to organize information teachers need to know and help maintain it in awareness, and 2) observational checklists and rating scales to give teachers the means to establish data-based assessments of their students and their own teaching performance. We gave examples of all the kinds of tools, and we gave hints on how to create one's own checklists and rating scales. Finally, we offered some suggestions for going beyond one's own set of skills to get help from others both within the school setting and beyond.

Discussion Questions

- What are minder checklists?
- What are observational tools, and how do they help teachers organize and understand the language competencies of their students?
- What are checklists, and what are rating scales? When and why should teachers use them?
- What kinds of errors are we most prone to make in using checklists and rating scales?

Chapter 6

Making and Using Comparisons of Languages and Language Use

Why Make Comparisons?

In Chapter 3, we described some of the ways languages can be alike and different. We also noted that there is more than one way to take on the task of learning second or third languages. Some learners rely on what they know of their first language to guide their learning of another; others take on learning the second language as a new challenge and report that they are, at least consciously, unencumbered by the old. We cannot definitively say which of these approaches is better. Many factors, such as the degree of learning of the first language, the scope of similarities and differences between first and second languages, the learning situation, and the predilections of the student as learner will influence the success of any given approach and the degree to which there is transfer from knowledge of one language to the learning of another.

However, we suspect that making explicit the various ways languages are structured does help. For one thing, teachers can gain insights about the aspects of English that English Language Learners (ELLs) may find most challenging. Such insights can be especially useful when dealing with students unaccustomed to academic language because such students may have difficulties with literacy tasks like spelling and understanding the complex language used in the disciplines. For another, students can acquire an understanding of language not just as an everyday ability but as an object of interest in itself. Students need to take pride in their dual-language status. Knowing where and why they may have trouble with English may help them to understand their own learning process better and to overcome obstacles in mastering it. Teachers are the instruments whereby students can gain such knowledge about themselves. For teachers to be able to fulfill that role, they need to have some understanding of the relation between English and their students' home languages and how earlier language experiences can impact learning English. But few teachers are or can be polyglots. Instead, to help teachers understand their students' situations, we created a set of charts, or tables, comparing English with other languages on a set of features that commonly present challenges for ELLs. These are presented below, but first we offer some comments on what we have included in the charts and how to use them.

There are more than 150 home languages represented among the nation's ELLs. We could not in this chapter suggest all the ways that all these home languages differ from English and how they may impact student errors. What we did instead was focus on a subset of languages that are among the most commonly represented in American public schools. The tables in this chapter represent eight languages and only one version of each of those eight at that, although many of the languages have multiple versions. For example, Spanish is spoken in various geographical areas and, although mutually intelligible, the various versions can differ in multiple ways. Also, French is the basis of several creoles, which nonetheless can be quite different from each other as well as from French.

We then drew on the experience and expertise of people who know at least one of the eight languages in addition to English. Whether native to English or to another language, all had insight into the differences and similarities that could present challenges for speakers of these languages when learning English. Ten consultants helped in the creation of the language comparison charts in this chapter. They made suggestions for a useful list of comparison features that may be implicated in many of the common errors made by ELLs from one of these language backgrounds. Importantly, they explained their language's characteristics for inclusion in the subsequent charts and made notations about possible problems (see columns 3 and 4, Tables 6.2–6.9).

The same list of features appears in the first column of each table from Table 6.1 to 6.9. Each table also includes in column 2 a short description of the value of that feature in English. Tables 6.2–6.9 include in column 3 "comparison language," a description of that feature's value in the comparison language; and column 4 "possible problem or error" for ELL, a description of the kind of problem that may occur for an ELL from that comparison language. In Table 6.1, columns 3 and 4 are left blank so that teachers may copy the table and fill it in for any language not found in Tables 6.2–6.9 but represented among their students. To keep the tables to a manageable size, we have made the feature descriptions relatively short and concise, necessarily ignoring details and various exceptions.

Choosing Languages and Features to Compare

It will come as no surprise to teachers that Spanish is the home language for over 70 percent of all ELLs. Data from the 2008–2009 Consolidated State Performance Reports (CSPR) show that Spanish is the home language for over 65 percent of them in each of twenty-eight states and for over 80 percent of them in thirteen of those states (www.migrationinformaton.org/ellinfo/FactSheet). Despite its overwhelming status as the most frequent home language among ELLs in the US, there are seven states in which Spanish is not the top home language, and there are ten states where no single language is the home language for even 50 percent of the ELLs in the state (although Spanish is still the most frequent home language in four of those states). Thus, these ten states have very heterogeneous ELLs, with many languages represented and no one of them dominant. It can be a mixed blessing for teachers when only one language is prevalent. In recent years, the focus has been on students whose home language is Spanish. On the one hand, then, there are readily available resources on Spanish and for teaching ELLs from that home language (although teachers need to keep in mind that there are geographically-based variations within the broad categories of Spanish language and culture). On the other hand, information on other languages can be harder to find. If teachers have classes with ELLs from a less well-known language background or with a heterogeneous ELL population, fewer language-specific resources may be available, and the task of helping each student becomes more difficult. We suggest that teachers check the data on their state on the relevant web sites listed in Appendix A so that they get a picture of the local demographics of ELLs. Also, Chapter 4 includes suggestions of where to get help.

Our sample languages and comparative features were selected for a variety of reasons. We wanted to illustrate a range of the kinds of errors that can occur among learners from the language backgrounds most commonly found in US schools. To identify the languages, we examined web sites of major school districts in the US, as well as searched websites on the most common languages in the US. We knew that we could not illustrate everything. Still, we wanted both our language choices and the features that we chose for comparison to English to be diverse enough so that many possible sources of error could be included, even if they were not likely to be problematic for speakers of a highly frequent home language like Spanish. For example, Spanish uses Latin script like English, but many others do not. As different as Russian, Korean, and Chinese are from one another, none uses Latin script; all children from those home languages share the task of learning Latin script as they learn to read and write English. Thus, we include type of script as one comparative feature. Similarly, within the bounds of relative commonality in the schools, we chose to include languages that were fairly representative of a group. For example, Russian and Polish share many features, but, in choosing only one, we chose Russian because it is a more common home language among current ELLs in schools. Our choices were also influenced by our consultants' expertise. Although rather different from one another, Bengali and Hindi are both important languages on the Indian subcontinent, and both are common heritage languages in US schools. We wanted to choose one of those to include here; we had available to us a consultant whose native language is Bengali, and so we chose to represent that.

It is important to note that over 10 percent of ELLs in US schools come from language backgrounds that are not among the top ten languages found in the schools. These include, for example, all the languages of Native Americans. In a few states (e.g., Alaska), those languages make up the majority of home

Table 6.1 Language Comparison Chart*

Language feature	English	Comparison language**	Possible problem or error for ELL
Syllable structure, e.g., are consonant clusters (c-c's) at starts or ends of words allowed? Does consonant-vowel (c-v) predominate? Is there dropping or eliding, or silent letters?	Frequent consonant clusters can be at start and end of words (e.g., str, scr, -lms): has silent letters, elisions, e.g., can't		
Are there borrowings or influences from other languages?	Germanic and Romance roots cause inconsistent spelling or pronunciation patterns, e.g., rough and ruff		
Word formation complexity scale goes from simple to midway to complex, e.g., monosyllabic (simple) to multisyllabic, with prefixes or suffixes (complex)	English is midway: it has many multisyllabic words; some grammatical markings, e.g., walk, walk-s; some adding of morphemes to roots to make new lexical items (e.g., nation, national)		
Misleading word translations: borrowed words or cognates may look similar but have different meanings, sometimes called "false friends"	Many languages borrow words from English but the meanings may change, e.g., in English, actual means real, the similar word means current in some other languages		
Are there gendered words? Is the basis natural? Grammatical?	Natural, only on pronouns (e.g., he, she)		
Articles: Where and when are they used? Are there consistent rules for use?	Rules for definites, generics, indefinites, mass and count nouns but inconsistent		

Language feature	English	Comparison language**	Possible problem or error for ELL
Spatial relations: how expressed	Prepositions: choice depends on meaning intended with particular verb used		
Does the copula (connecting verb) appear in present tense? In other tenses?	Yes, *be*, e.g., *I am good; I am hungry; I was hungry.* Past, present, and future tenses		
Are there auxiliary verbs?	Yes, required in some constructions, but some dialect variation in how they are used		
Are there verb particles?	Yes, e.g., *turn off*		
How are questions formed?	Auxiliary inversion (*do* if needed), Q words, e.g., *Are you going? Do you want a drink? What time is it?*		
How are commands and requests formed?	Direct imperatives, e.g., *Close the door;* indirect directives, e.g., *Can you ...; Why don't you ...;* very indirect requests, e.g., *It's noisy in the hall* (meaning *close the door*)		
Scale of verb marking: none–some–many; consistent?	Some, e.g.: *-s, -ed, -ing.* Some irregularities, e.g., *went*		
Scale of noun marking: none–few–some–many; consistent?	Some: case marking on pronouns, e.g., *I, me, they, them;* possessive *–'s,* plural *–s,* some irregularities, e.g., *two deer*		

Table 6.1 Continued

Language feature	English	Comparison language**	Possible problem or error for ELL
Is there subject–verb agreement?	For singular and plural only, e.g., *He goes, we go*		
What is the type and importance, and consistency, of word order?	SVO; fairly important and consistent		
Is subject dropping allowed?	Not allowed; dummy *it*, e.g., *It's raining*		
Formality scale: casual–mixed–formal language, e.g., forms of address and use of names; gendered or age-based styles?	Mixed, but tending to casual: slang, everyday speech; but academic language; no formal age- or gender-based styles		
Indirect speech scale, amount of hedging: none–some–much	Much, e.g., *I think . . ., maybe*		
Does the student engage in classroom talk?	Participates, asks and answers questions, engages in discussions		
Writing system	Alphabetic, Latin script		
Is there a written language style?	More formal, academic; different styles for different purposes		

* Features of languages and possible problems are based on general descriptions and ignore exceptional details.
** Columns 3 and 4 are left blank on this chart so that teachers can copy this chart and fill it in for any language represented in their classes but not included in charts 6.2–6.9.

languages of a state's ELLs, but across the nation they are relatively small in number; we do not include any here in the charts. However, teachers of such "minority" ELL languages can benefit from examining the features we discuss and following suggestions for making charts of their own.

Our final list of languages included Arabic, Bengali, Chinese, French, Hmong, Korean, Russian, and Spanish. Each of the tables 6.2 through 6.9 compares English with one of our eight languages on the same set of features.

Teachers are encouraged to use the tables as guides to the kinds of errors they may see. When we had specific information about errors, we included it. When we did not, we gave a range of possible errors or entered a question mark. Blank cells indicate that problems are unlikely. Because not all languages found in the schools are represented, the tables should be taken as examples of the kinds of tables teachers can create themselves for the particular languages represented and the kinds of errors made by the ELLs in their classrooms. As we noted earlier, teachers should feel free to copy Table 6.1 as needed and fill it out for whatever languages are represented in their classroom. Web sites suggested in Appendix A can help with that task. There is more on how to use the tables in a later section.

The Eight Languages

With the help of our language consultants, we provide in the following paragraphs some background information on each of the languages.

Arabic

Arabic is the official language of twenty-six countries and has an estimated 200 million speakers. However, it is a broad term for a language with many mutually unintelligible dialects. For many native speakers, their ability to use the Standard Arabic dialect of schools, newspapers, and media may be limited. Regional dialects are not written and have low status in the eyes of many speakers. Most native speakers learn a regional dialect at home and only begin to learn Standard Arabic in school. Depending on level of education, some people may attain only a passive knowledge of Standard Arabic and not ever master speaking or writing it. Additionally, the countries whose official language is Arabic are home to hundreds of linguistic minorities. These children may learn a different, unrelated, language at home and only learn Arabic at school, making them second language speakers of both the dialect and the formal registers.

Bengali

Bengali (also known as Bangla) is an Indo-Aryan language spoken in eastern India and the country of Bangladesh. In terms of the number of speakers, it ranks fifth or sixth among the world's languages. It is the national and official language of Bangladesh and is one of the recognized regional languages of India. There are substantial Bengali communities in the US, Europe, Australia, and the Middle East. It resembles other Indo-Aryan languages and has borrowed heavily from Sanskrit, Persian, Arabic, and English. It has a very rich literary history and has contributed much to Indian literature for many years.

Chinese

Standard Chinese (also known as Beijing Mandarin, Mandarin Chinese, or simply Mandarin) is the official spoken language of China, Taiwan (where it is called *Guoyu*, "National Language") and Singapore (where it is called *Huayu*, "Chinese Language"). It is one of over 100 dialects spoken in China and is used by over 845 million people worldwide. More than a billion people speak one of the various dialects of Chinese, which are generally mutually intelligible. While Standard Chinese is based on the Beijing dialect, most Chinese can speak, read, and write in Standard Chinese even if it is not their native dialect.

French

French is a Romance language spoken in France, parts of Switzerland and Belgium, parts of Canada (i.e., Quebec), and former colonies in Africa, Asia, the Americas, the Indian Ocean, and the Caribbean among other places. France's colonial history gave rise to a number of French-based creoles that typically emerged in the 17th century from contact between non-standard varieties of the French language and African and/or Amerindian languages. These creoles include Haitian Creole (which has by far the largest number of speakers, estimated to 12 million), Lesser Antillean (Martinique, Guadeloupe, St Lucia) in the Caribbean, Louisiana Creole in the US, Mauritian Creole, Reunionnais Creole, and Seychellois in the Indian Ocean, to name just a few.

Hmong

Hmong is a Southeast Asian language of the Hmong-Mien language family of southern China and northern Southeast Asia (Vietnam, Laos, and Thailand). The Hmong in the US came from Laos originally; they were resettled in the West in a number of migrations following the Vietnam War. Hmong in the US currently number about 260,000; the greatest population concentrations are in California, Minnesota, Wisconsin, and North Carolina. Most young Hmong students in the schools will have been born in the US and therefore usually speak English fluently; they typically serve as translators for the older members of their families who were born in Laos. They will probably not be proficient in formal, Academic English, however. Adult Hmong students will tend to have the kinds of problems noted in the chart.

Korean

Korean is spoken by about 78 million people worldwide. It is the official language of both North and South Korea, but with mutually intelligible dialects. The language lacks some grammatical elements found in English, in particular, articles and relative pronouns. For Korean ELLs, both consonant and vowel distinctions can be problematic. Stress is not important in Korean, and so Korean students' English may sound flat to native English speakers. The distinction between formal and informal speech in Korean is age-based and explicit, in contrast to the more subtle distinctions in English.

Russian

Russian is a member of the Slavic language family, which includes, among others, Ukrainian, Belarusian, Czech, Slovak, Polish, Bulgarian, Macedonian, Serbian, and Croatian. Slavic languages are spoken throughout much of Eastern Europe, the Balkans, and parts of Central Europe. They typically use either a Cyrillic or Latin alphabet. The former includes Latin, Greek, and Hebrew letters. After the revolution of 1917, the previously erratic spelling of Russian was revised to be highly regular and phonetic.

Spanish

Spanish, a member of the Romance language family, is the official language of Spain, of nineteen republics in Central and South America as well as the Caribbean, and of Equatorial Guinea. There are over 400 million people who claim Spanish as their first language. It has become the second language of the US with over 30 million speakers. The various differences between European and non–European standard varieties of Spanish are relatively minimal and do not affect mutual intelligibility, but teachers should be aware that there are some differences in vocabulary and syntax.

Criteria for Selecting Features for the Tables

We had several criteria for selecting features for our tables. First, we wanted an array of features to illustrate the point that any of the various components of language and language use may cause problems; we did not want to focus on only, say, vocabulary. Second, because we wanted a single feature list of manageable size, we wanted to include features whose values illustrate common, often trouble-causing, differences not just between two languages, but across many languages. For example, English uses the copula *be*, but many other languages do not (at least in the present tense), and speakers of such languages often mistakenly drop it in English. Third, some aspects of English, for example, articles, are difficult for virtually all ELLs, whatever their home language, and we wanted to represent such features. Fourth, we wanted features we could describe concisely in table form with a minimum of technical terminology. That is, we wanted the tables to be practical: they had to be accessible to teachers with minimal preparation in language study and of usable size. The resulting list of twenty-two features and their English values is found in the first two columns of Table 6.1 and repeated in condensed form in Tables 6.2 through 6.9. Of course, such a comparative feature list could be both much longer and more specific. There are many details and exceptions that we could not hope to cover using this format. Nonetheless, we hope that what we have developed will be useful to teachers in their work with ELLs from a variety of backgrounds, as well as help them understand some of the complexities of languages and their differences.

Beyond the Tables

In this section, we describe three important sources of language differences that are not fully reflected in the tables. The first is differences in sound systems, the second concerns literacy and cultural differences in written genres, and the third refers to the issue of consistency in language systems, particularly those having to do with aspects of grammar.

Sound Systems

One of the gaps in the tables that may strike the reader at first glance is that the tables have little information about sound systems beyond *syllable structure.* The reason for this is that describing sound systems and all the phonemic differences across languages that are found there is a daunting task, not easily accomplished without the use of much technical terminology (and many more pages). For example, English has a large system of vowels, and speakers of languages with smaller systems may find the larger system difficult. Similarly, languages can be very different with regard to the consonantal distinctions they make. For example, a familiar problem for Spanish ELLs is the one caused by the *b-v* distinction in English but not Spanish (except in the spelling of some words in Spanish). Another example, this one often presenting difficulty for English speakers learning Arabic, is the distinction in Arabic between different kinds of the *k* sound. To represent sound systems in the tables, we chose the general case of syllable structure and used the occurrence of consonant clusters (*c-c*'s) as an instance of possible differences. We did so because those languages not allowing *c-c*'s deal with words borrowed from English in such compelling ways. For example, inserting a vowel between every consonant in a cluster to create separate syllables turns the English word *strike* (as in *throw a strike to a batter*) into *su-to-ri-ku* in Japanese, which requires *c-v* syllables. As this example so clearly illustrates, transitioning between sound systems may produce problems for pronunciation, spelling, and even comprehension. Although we could not catalog all of them here, teachers need to be attentive to such problems and their possible origins.

Literacy

Another instance of difference that cannot be fully explicated in the tables is related to literacy in English. Both reading and writing require an understanding of the structure and style of various genres. However, a culture's values can be reflected in its texts, via content, style, or structure, thereby resulting in differences between English texts and those in other languages. Such differences are found even in picture books translated into various languages (Shatz, *et al.*, 2006). The differences can be subtle, influencing, for example, how interpersonal relations are conveyed and are to be interpreted. Although they learn about the various genres in English in American schools, ELLs who have been exposed to another culture's ways of creating and comprehending text may have difficulty adapting to English content, styles, and structures. ELL students may need to be explicitly encouraged to attend to such potential differences.

Consistency

The theme of *consistency* cuts across many of the features in the table. Research on first language learners confirms that children reveal a preference for consistency. There are numerous examples in the language acquisition literature of young children preferring one-meaning-to-one-form mappings or regular endings for, say, past tenses. A language like English can be inconsistent in how and when it marks something (or how it relates pronunciation to spelling). This can be difficult for a second language learner whose first language may be more consistent, either because it always marks features such as plural or it never does. Such a learner may incorrectly infer English is also consistent one way or the other, thereby either over-using markings or under-using them. Thus, differences in consistency of marking between first and later-learned languages can itself be a cause for error.

Note too that inconsistency can result either from having a rule that is applied to only part of a feature (like subject–verb agreement) or from having no overt rule for a feature that can be taught. For example, English has a rule for marking third-person singular agreement on a verb with –*s*. Apart from the verb *be* with singular pronouns, that is the only overt number–person agreement in English. The rule may be somewhat difficult for learners coming from languages with more consistent subject–verb agreement across all persons, but it still is a rule that can be taught. In contrast, consider the case of articles and when to use them. In English a singular noun can be used as a *generic* (to refer to a whole class), but a generic noun sometimes takes an article and sometimes does not, e.g., *the lion is the king of beasts*, but *death comes to all men*. We cannot cite a specific rule for when to use the article with generic nouns. Little wonder that many ELLs report so much trouble with when to use articles even after years of studying English.

Expanding on the Features

In this section, we give some additional information about only those features in the tables that we deemed in need of more explanation for readers to understand them.

Syllable Structure

As noted above, languages vary greatly in terms of the meaningful sound distinctions they make as well as how they cluster those sounds. Some languages have only single-syllable words (e.g., Vietnamese), some have simple consonant–vowel composition for every syllable (e.g., Japanese), and some end every word with the same syllable (e.g., Hmong). In contrast, English has multi-syllabic words, complex consonant clusters, and a wide variety of sounds at word-end. Such differences can make for difficulties in comprehending and producing spoken language. Moreover, there are implications for such differences when it comes to moving from speaking to reading. We tend to be much more forgiving of language errors as listeners (when we can ask for clarification) than we are as readers.

Borrowing

Borrowing from other languages is of course a source of vitality for languages; it is what keeps so many ancient languages like Bengali functional in the 21st century. But, as the history of English attests, the result can be inconsistency in spelling and pronunciation patterns. These can be daunting even for first language learners (e.g., *b-v* in Spanish), but can be especially so for ELLs, whose home language may have different sources of borrowed words as well as different ways of adapting them to the home language's sound system. (See "Word Translations" below for difficulties with the meanings of borrowed words.)

Word Formation

Closely related to the topic of syllable structure is the question of whether and how a language adds to its basic words: does it attach pieces to words to add or change meanings or grammatical information? Or do those pieces stand alone? For example, in English, one can attach what are called grammatical morphemes like -*ed* to a verb to refer to the past. But, in some languages, the past would be regularly marked with a separate, typically small, separate word. (We can even do both in English, e.g., "*she smiled, she did smile,*" but the latter is used more rarely, only for emphasis.) One can also add pieces before or after a root word to change the meaning and/or grammatical category of a word, for example, turning the word *nature* into *un-natur(e)-al*. The word formation scale is a way of describing how much a language allows attaching morphemes together to make larger units, going from simple languages that do very little attaching pieces together to those that fall in the middle (midway) to those that do a lot (complex).

Word Translations

Some words in other languages may have similar looking or sounding counterparts to English words. One reason for this is that two languages may be cognate; that is, they share a common ancestor that has influenced the vocabulary in both languages. So, English *beam* is cognate to German *baum* (*tree*) (Matthews, 2007). Another reason is that, as English has increased in its importance as an international language, many languages borrow words, especially technical words, from it. Virtually all ELLs come to the learning of English with a store of such words. Unfortunately, the meanings of such cognates or borrowings may be transformed in subtle ways such that words that look alike do not necessarily mean the same thing in each language; hence, the name they have been given of "false friends." ELLs can be forewarned about such. (See Swan & Smith, 2001, for many examples.) Also, it is important that both teachers and students realize that translations are virtually never word for word. Style, cultural values, and grammatical differences between languages all contribute to changes from one language to another, making comprehending written language as well as speaking another language a real challenge.

Gender

English refers to *natural genders* of male and female with different pronouns (e.g., *she*, *he*). It is acceptable to refer to an animal (but not a person) as the neuter *it*, which is used for other entities. Other languages (like German) may use what is called *grammatical gender* for all nouns. Still other languages follow natural gender for animates but arbitrarily assign masculine or feminine gender to inanimates. For example, in Spanish, *the key* is feminine (*la llave*) and *the train* is masculine (*el tren*). Some languages include a neuter; the noun for, say, *table* could be marked as masculine, feminine, neuter, or not marked for gender at all, depending on the language. Pronouns (and often articles, adjectives, and verbs) agree with the gender of the noun (e.g., *la belle Hélène* but *le beau Jean* in French). Thus, languages can vary from no gender markings at all to markings throughout different parts of the language.

Spatial Relations

English uses prepositions such as *in*, *on*, and *under* to express spatial relations between objects. It also tends to use distinct words like *out* and *in* to describe what are called *path* or locational characteristics. So, for example, while English does have verbs like *exit*, it is more customary to use the phrase *go out*. In some languages, spatial relationships are expressed differently; for example, Spanish prefers verbs like *exit* for expressing path. Also, spatial words can refer to different or additional aspects of a relation (e.g., not just whether an object is in a container, but the degree of fit of the object in the container, such as, in Korean, a hand in a glove, Bowerman & Choi, 2001).

Auxiliary Verbs

Auxiliary or modal verbs like *may*, *must*, *can*, and *will* do a variety of work in English, such as changing an action from reality to possibility or from present to future. Other languages may do this work in a variety of other ways. Even those that use some form of auxiliary verbs may not handle the main verb the same way English does. For example, English does not use the infinitival *to* with auxiliaries nor does it mark person on the main verb (e.g., *He may go*; not *He may to go* or *He may goes*). Moreover, a modal verb like *must*, and its counterpart in other languages, can have multiple interpretations (e.g., obligation or certainty); the prevalence of one interpretation over the other in the home language may influence how the modal is interpreted in English (Shatz, 1991).

Questions, Commands, and Requests

All languages must express the various communicative functions of making statements, asking questions, and making demands. They can accomplish this work differently, however. Intonation can be important, as can intensity, especially for commands, but there can also be devices more internal to the structure of the language, such as particular words or word orders. In English, commands and requests can be especially subtle; for example, the question form can be used when a request or command is intended (e.g., *Could you turn in your homework on time in the future?*). Thus, constructions can convey different intentions depending on the context in which they are used.

An anecdote from a trip we took to Japan years ago illustrates well our points about the possible misinterpretation of modal verbs and indirect forms. We had been taken to a restaurant in Tokyo by a former graduate student and were being treated to dish after dish of expensive foods. The abundant array was much more than we could manage to consume, and, as still more food arrived, one of us said, "Oh, you mustn't!" Our host's face fell, and we realized that, rather than expressing our gratitude at her generosity, she thought we disapproved and were criticizing her. We hurried to assure her we were very pleased with her graciousness.

Scales of Marking

Grammatical gender agreement discussed above is one example of how a language might accrue a lot of marking on various parts of speech. The tables' rows on scales of verb and noun marking and on subject–verb agreement all refer to differences among languages in how much they mark for plurality, gender, and semantic role (e.g., subject, object, possessive), and how consistent they are in doing so. As noted earlier, English is notoriously inconsistent in its use of markings; indeed, some experts now group it with languages like Chinese that rarely if ever use grammatical markings.

Word Order and Subject Dropping

As discussed in Chapter 3, languages can differ in word order. They also differ in the importance of word order for comprehension. Typically, there is a trade-off: languages that have a lot of grammatical markings (i.e., are high on the scales of marking) rely less on word order for comprehension, so word order can be freer. Recall the subject dropping example in Chapter 3 of highly marked Italian, *piove*; subject dropping can be done only when there is a way of identifying the dropped element. So, languages that are high on marking (or that use discourse devices like Chinese) can do it. English cannot.

Language Use

All languages have different ways of talking in different circumstances. Some rely on very explicit forms to be used to signal politeness or respect for age or status. Some languages like English signal informality or equality by hedging commands with phrases like *I think* (e.g., *I think it's bedtime* instead of *Go to bed*). Our formality and indirect speech scales try to capture the kinds of socially based variations found in the uses of different languages. It is worth noting that more than specific devices (e.g., *sir, madam*) influence the character of language use. Languages are used in social contexts, and the contexts themselves influence interpretation. Even in English, an utterance meant to be interpreted one way in a given context can be intended to be taken quite differently in another. For example, in one context, asking the question, "Do you know what time it is?" may be a request, even from a stranger, to be told the time; in a different context, it may be an exhortation from one partner to another about getting to an appointment promptly. Note that in neither context would a simple yes/no answer to the literal question be appropriate. Cultures differ on the norms for when it is appropriate to use direct or literal speech. For example, in Arabic the use of direct requests and imperatives to elders is considered impolite.

Writing

Many of the world's languages do not use Latin script, and some are not even alphabetic. These differences add another layer of complexity to the task of acquiring literacy in English. Writing involves two other problems as well. First, as noted in the section on literacy above, different cultures have different styles and structures for writing, so writing in English for academic purposes may be quite different from what an ELL may have experienced in another setting. Also, for all students, writing is very different from face-to-face, two-way communication in that there is no feedback and no means to assess ongoing understanding. Due to cultural differences, ELL writers may face even more of a challenge than other students because they may be unable to assume as much about what their English readers are like and what they know.

How to Use the Comparison Charts

Teachers should approach the following charts only after reading the above sections as background for interpreting them and for help in understanding the charts' necessarily concise entries. These charts are intended as tools to help teachers identify the possible problems and their sources that ELLs with varied language experiences may have.

General education teachers can use the language comparison charts to identify pronunciation, spelling, grammar, and vocabulary errors that their ELL students may be more likely to make. These charts can be used before, during, and after a lesson. For example, during the planning of a lesson, the chart can assist teachers in predicting errors or misconceptions that ELLs may make. Teachers can utilize these predictions as a basis to prepare a lesson that is accessible for all the students in the class, making alterations for ELL students as required. In addition, teachers can showcase what language proficiency ELL students do have by planning and eliciting communication sequences where they can use those strengths.

The language comparison charts may also be used as an efficient way to identify and then classify errors in ELLs' oral or written language productions as linked either to a language feature or to lesson content. When doing so, teachers can address the error immediately or reserve the corrections for a later private conversation or a one-to-one tutoring session. For example, with regard to classroom talk, a student from an Arabic-speaking culture, accustomed primarily to rote learning and not familiar with the activity structures (such as inquiry circles) commonly found in US classrooms, may be reluctant to initiate or engage in discussions. Moreover, because of politeness considerations in the home culture, he or she may be reluctant to ask questions or make direct requests of a teacher or older student. The teacher could address the differences between Arabic and English custom in the classroom with a quiet, encouraging aside to the student that it is fine in the US classroom to use direct requests and to participate in all classroom activities, including discussions.

All teachers can use the charts to assess and reflect on their lesson after implementation. They can make notes on an ELL's errors or misconceptions regarding language features or area content and discern a potential root of the error and potential directed intervention. Thereby, they can use these language comparison charts to enhance their understanding about why an ELL student may be making particular mistakes or pattern of mistakes in either oral or written language, or both. One of our reviewers made the excellent suggestion that the charts could even be shown to particular ELLs (from late elementary school years) who speak those languages to help them gain insight into their own English-learning challenges (E. McNulty, personal communication, November 15, 2011).

We have suggested that teachers construct their own charts for languages they encounter that are not covered in this chapter. When they do so, they may need to consult the resources posted in Appendix A, and/or confer with ESL teachers or other colleagues in refugee/settlement centers, or language/linguistics departments at nearby colleges and universities. We also suggest that teachers may want to add a fifth column to the charts with the heading "*Possible solution.*" Teachers can then enter their own ideas (possibly in consultation with other teachers or specialists) about how to help a particular student or solve a particular problem. After trying out an idea, they can make a note about its success and later share successful strategies with colleagues.

Finally, these eight language comparison charts of some of the most frequently occurring home languages for US ELL students will help general education teachers recognize the complex and inconsistent nature of English.

Table 6.2 Arabic*

Language feature	English	Arabic	Possible problem or error
Syllable structure, e.g., consonant clusters (c-c's) at starts or ends of words allowed? Consonant–vowel (c-v)? Dropping, eliding, silent letters?	Frequent consonant clusters can be at start and end of words (e.g., str-, scr-, -lms); has silent letters, elisions, e.g., can't	Consonant clusters possible, but not as long as in English; p is not a sound in Arabic	Pronunciation and spelling; often replaces p with b in speaking
Borrowing or influences from other languages	Germanic and Romance roots cause inconsistent spelling or pronunciation patterns, e.g., rough and ruff	Borrowings from French and English, but often heavily adapted to Arabic sound system	Words of English or French origin may be pronounced according to Arabic sound system.
Word formation complexity scale: simple–midway–complex, e.g., monosyllabic (simple) to multisyllabic, prefixes or suffixes (complex)	Midway: some grammatical markings, e.g., walk, walk-s; some new lexical items (e.g., nation, national)	Complex: prefixes and suffixes; number, person, gender markings. Most words built on three-consonant root, with varied patterns changing meanings; plural markings inconsistent and unpredictable	The English word formation system is less patterned than Arabic, so finding connections between related words in English may be hard for native Arabic speakers
Misleading word translations; "false friends"	E.g., in English, actual means real, but current in some other languages	Not many because of the word-derivation system	Little to none
Gendered words: Natural? Grammatical?	Natural, only on pronouns (e.g., he, she)	M and f marked on all verbs, adjectives, and many nouns, but f not always overtly marked	Incorrect use of gendered pronouns to refer to inanimate objects

Language feature	English	Arabic	Possible problem or error
Articles: where and when to use; consistency	Rules for definites, generics, indefinites, mass and count nouns but inconsistent	Definite always marked, indefinite usually marked in writing, more rarely in speech. Generics and mass nouns can take definite	Definite marking on generics and mass nouns
Spatial relations: how expressed?	Prepositions: choice depends on meaning intended with particular verb used	Preposition used can completely change verb meaning. Some attach directly to the following word	Wrong word choice
Copula (connecting verb)?	Yes, be, e.g., I am hungry; I was hungry. Past, present, and future tenses	No copula in the present tense, often omitted in future, but required in the past tense	Missing copula or future not marked, e.g., He good, I buy tomorrow.
Auxiliary verbs?	Yes, some dialect variation	Yes, but dialect variation. Passives, conditionals, and future tense sometimes marked other ways	May be used differently or omitted where expected in English
Verb particles?	Yes, e.g., turn off	Yes	
Forming questions	Aux inversion, Q words, do, e.g., Are you going? What time is it? Do you want a drink?	Q word mainly in literary Arabic; inversion mostly in spoken Arabic	Do omission, with inversion and intonation as question markers
Commands and requests	Direct imperatives; indirect directives, e.g., Can you . . ., Why don't you . . .; very indirect requests, e.g., It's noisy in the hall (meaning Close the door)	Direct imperatives as in English; a polite form of address in imperatives is possible. Direct requests to elders considered impolite	Misinterpretation of speaker intent

Table 6.2 Continued

Language feature	English	Arabic	Possible problem or error
Scale of verb marking: none–some–many. Consistent?	Some, e.g., -s, -ed, -ing. Some irregularities, e.g., went	Verbs have unvarying markings for number, person, and gender in present tense	English irregular verbs may cause problems at first
Scale of noun marking: none–few–some–many. Consistent?	Some: case marking on pronouns, e.g., I, me, they, them; possessives, -s, plural -s. Some irregularities, e.g., two deer	Plural and feminine markers. Objects directly attached to the verb instead of as stand-alone pronouns	May have some trouble initially with object pronouns
Subject–verb agreement	For singular and plural	For singular, plural, and dual, but number on the verb depends on verb's position in sentence	Possible trouble with subject–verb agreement if the verb not in its canonical place in English
Type and importance, and consistency of word order	SVO; fairly important and consistent	Spoken Arabic generally SVO; literary Arabic starts main clauses with V	Some verbs may appear at the beginning of sentences
Subject dropping allowed?	Not allowed; dummy it, e.g., It's raining	Yes	Missing subject pronouns
Formality scale: casual–mixed–formal language (e.g., forms of address and use of names); gendered or age-based styles?	Mixed, tending to casual: slang, everyday speech, academic language; no formal age- or gender-based styles	Formal terms of address for respect; for mixed-gender groups, all agreement is M	

Language feature	English	Arabic	Possible problem or error
Indirect speech scale, amount of hedging: none–some–much	Much, e.g., *I think . . ., maybe*	Much hedging, e.g., the phrase God-willing when agreeing to act	
Classroom talk	Participates, asks and answers questions, engages in discussions	Possibly more rote memorization and less discussion and questioning	Possible reluctance to participate in discussion
Writing system	Alphabetic, Latin script	Alphabetic, but short vowels omitted. Right-to-left Arabic script. No case distinctions; punctuation rare	Concepts of printing, punctuation, and distinguishing between upper and lower cases may be difficult
Written language	More formal, academic; different styles for different purposes	Very formal, requiring high levels of education for mastery. Formal Arabic considered a holy language and art form. Spoken dialects considered "debased" forms of standard	Speakers of dialects without formal education in Arabic may lack experience with written forms of language

* Features of languages and possible problems are based on general descriptions and ignore exceptional details. See Table 6.1 for fuller descriptions of columns 1 and 2.

Table 6.3 Bengali*

Language feature	English	Bengali (Bangla)	Possible problem or error
Syllable structure, e.g., consonant clusters (c-c's) at starts or ends of words allowed? Consonant–vowel (c-v)? Dropping, eliding, silent letters?	Frequent consonant clusters can be at start and end of words (e.g., str-, scr-, -lms); has silent letters, elisions, e.g., can't	Complex syllables allowed, like CCCVC. Syllable onsets can be complex. No silent letters or elision	Some consonant clusters of English are not allowed in Bengali. These can lead to problems in pronunciation
Borrowing or influences from other languages	Germanic and Romance roots cause inconsistent spelling or pronunciation patterns, e.g., rough and ruff	Lots of borrowings from English. Code-switching between English and Bengali is rampant	Influence of English on Bengali may facilitate learning English
Word formation complexity scale: simple–midway–complex, e.g., monosyllabic (simple) to multisyllabic, prefixes or suffixes (complex)	Midway: some grammatical markings, e.g., walk, walk-s; some new lexical items (e.g., nation, national)	Complex: grammatical (tense, number) endings on verbs; complex nouns can be derived from adjectives	
	Learners may over-use some derivational processes of English to derive new words		
Misleading word translations; "false friends"	E.g., in English, actual means real, but current in some other languages	Some borrowed words have incorrect usage	Incorrect usage may influence vocabulary learning in English
Gendered words: Natural? Grammatical?	Natural, only on pronouns (e.g., he, she)	Natural gender, but not marked even on pronouns	Incorrect gender choices of pronouns

Language feature	English	Bengali (Bangla)	Possible problem or error
Articles: where and when to use; consistency	Rules for definites, generics, indefinites, mass and count nouns but inconsistent	Numericals used instead of articles. Use of demonstratives after nouns to refer to definite.	Post-posing instead of pre-posing of demonstratives; omitting articles
Spatial relations: how expressed	Prepositions: choice depends on meaning intended with particular verb used	Use of post positions instead of prepositions	Possible wrong word choice; possible position error
Copula (connecting verb)?	Yes, be, e.g., *I am good; I am hungry; I was hungry.* Past, present, and future tenses	No copulas	Missing copula, e.g., *He good*
Auxiliary verbs?	Yes, some dialect variation	Auxiliaries used after main verbs	Possible position problem
Verb particles?	Yes, e.g., *turn off*	Complex system of compound verbs; two verbs to express one action	Deciding which particle to use with which verb
Forming questions	Aux inversion, Q words, *do*, e.g., *Are you going? What time is it? Do you want a drink?*	As in English, but Q word not always at the beginning of sentence	Possible problem with the placement of Q word
Commands and requests	Direct imperatives; indirect directives, e.g., *Can you . . .*, *Why don't you . . .*; very indirect requests, e.g., *It's noisy in the hall* (meaning *Close the door*)	Use of both direct and indirect (impersonal) requests (e.g., use of passive constructions to indicate requests)	Misinterpretation of speaker intent

Table 6.3 Continued

Language feature	English	Bengali (Bangla)	Possible problem or error
Scale of verb marking: none–some–many. Consistent?	Some, e.g., -s, -ed, -ing. Some irregularities, e.g., went	Verbs inflected for tense, aspect, and person. Consistent	Irregularities in English verbs may be difficult to learn
Scale of noun marking: none–few–some–many. Consistent?	Some: case marking on pronouns, e.g., I, me, they, them; possessives, -s, plural —s. Some irregularities, e.g., two deer	Some; case markings on nouns and pronouns	?
Subject–verb agreement	For singular and plural	For person	?
Type and importance, and consistency of word order	SVO; fairly important and consistent	SOV word order. But word order is fairly flexible	Possible odd word orders
Subject dropping allowed?	Not allowed; dummy it, e.g., It's raining	Allowed	Subject omission
Formality scale: casual–mixed–formal language (e.g., forms of address and use of names); gendered or age-based styles?	Mixed, tending to casual: slang, everyday speech, academic language; no formal age- or gender-based styles	Distinction between informal and formal speech	
Indirect speech scale, amount of hedging: none–some–much	Much, e.g., I think . . ., maybe	Use of impersonal constructions very common. Non-nominative case marking on subjects to indicate impersonal constructions	Over-use of passive

Language feature	English	Bengali (Bangla)	Possible problem or error
Classroom talk	Participates, asks and answers questions, engages in discussions	Restrained, shy	Lack of participation
Writing system	Alphabetic, Latin script	Bengali script	
Written language	More formal, academic; different styles for different purposes	Informal and academic writing	

* Features of languages and possible problems are based on general descriptions and ignore exceptional details. See Table 6.1 for fuller descriptions of columns 1 and 2.

Table 6.4 Chinese*

Language feature	English	Standard Chinese (SC)	Possible problem or error
Syllable structure, e.g., consonant clusters (c-c's) at starts or ends of words allowed? Consonant–vowel (c-v)? Dropping, eliding, silent letters?	Frequent consonant clusters can be at start and end of words (e.g., str-, scr-, -lms); has silent letters, elisions, e.g., can't	No consonant clusters are allowed at starts and ends of words; the only consonants that can occur at the ends of words are –n and [ŋ] (ng)	Pronunciation: final consonant dropped (e.g., relac for relax); adding vowels after final consonant or inserting vowels between consonants
Borrowing or influences from other languages	Germanic and Romance roots cause inconsistent spelling or pronunciation patterns, e.g., rough and ruff	Transcription system (used in teaching) of SC has consistent spelling and pronunciation correspondences	Pronunciation and spelling: e.g., rough pronounced as rug; craft spelled as kraft
Word formation complexity scale: simple–midway–complex, e.g., monosyllabic (simple) to multisyllabic, prefixes or suffixes (complex)	Midway: some grammatical markings, e.g., walk, walk-s; some new lexical items (e.g., nation, national)	Simple: no such word formation	Under-use of grammatical markings, e.g., He walk home. Over- or mis-use of lexical affixes, e.g., contrastly, unuseful, uncomplete
Misleading word translations; "false friends"	E.g., in English, actual means real, but current in some other languages	Borrowed word may look or sound much the same but has a different (but often related) meaning	Collocation errors, e.g., large rain, hot regards, learn knowledge
Gendered words: Natural? Grammatical?	Natural, only on pronouns (e.g., he, she)	Natural, in written form (three different symbols for pronouns), but none in spoken language (all three pronounced the same)	Confusion over gendered pronouns, e.g., He is my sister

Language feature	English	Standard Chinese (SC)	Possible problem or error
Articles: where and when to use; consistency	Rules for definites, generics, indefinites, mass and count nouns but inconsistent	No articles	Misuse of articles, e.g., *He likes movie; He gained the weight last month*
Spatial relations: how expressed	Prepositions: choice depends on meaning intended with particular verb used	One-to-many mapping of prepositions from Chinese to English	Wrong word choice, e.g., *In a hot morning*; misuse, e.g., *Go to home*
Copula (connecting verb)?	Yes, *be*, e.g., *I am good; I am hungry; I was hungry*. Past, present, and future tenses	No copula	Missing copula, e.g., *I happy*
Auxiliary verbs?	Yes, some dialect variation	No auxiliary verbs	Omission of auxiliary verbs
Verb particles?	Yes, e.g., *turn off*	No verb particles	Difficulty learning and using such terms
Forming questions	Aux inversion, Q words, *do*, e.g., *Are you going? What time is it? Do you want a drink?*	Q words but no inversion, no *do*	Do omission, e.g., *How much you pay for your car?* No inversion, intonation only, e.g., *When you going home?*
Commands and requests	Direct imperatives; indirect directives, e.g., *Can you . . ., Why don't you . . .*; very indirect requests, e.g., *It's noisy in the hall* (meaning *Close the door*)	Similar distinctions between direct and indirect directives. Direct requests may be preferred more than in English	Misinterpretation of speaker intent; can be confused by the very indirect requests and not acknowledge speaker intent
Scale of verb marking: none–some–many. Consistent?	Some, e.g., *-s, -ed, -ing*. Some irregularities, e.g., *went*	None	Missing verb markings, e.g., *Yesterday I run*

Table 6.4 Continued

Language feature	English	Standard Chinese (SC)	Possible problem or error
Scale of noun marking: none–few–some–many. Consistent?	Some: case marking on pronouns, e.g., I, me, they, them; possessives, -s, plural-s. Some irregularities, e.g. two deer	None; possessives are represented by a particle	Confusion with pronouns, missing noun markings, e.g., I saw he; I have two brother
Subject–verb agreement	For singular and plural	None	Number disagreement, e.g., He like cheese; These is called . . .
Type and importance, and consistency of word order	SVO; fairly important and consistent	SVO; relative clause placed before noun; time and location placed before verbs	Difficulty using English relative clauses, e.g., I in China studied English for two years
Subject dropping allowed?	Not allowed; dummy it, e.g., It's raining	Allowed	Dropping of subjects
Formality scale: casual–mixed–formal language (e.g., forms of address and use of names); gendered or age-based styles?	Mixed, tending to casual: slang, everyday speech, academic language; no formal age- or gender-based styles	No gender-based styles. Some honorific/humble terms, e.g., honorific you and ordinary you; last name + job title as term of address, e.g., Smith teacher	Addressing people as "manager, teacher . . ."
Indirect speech scale, amount of hedging: none–some–much	Much, e.g., I think . . . maybe	Much, as in English	May be limited by vocabulary
Classroom talk	Participates, asks and answers questions, engages in discussions	Similar to those of English	May need more encouragement for participation; prefer small-groups discussion
Writing system	Alphabetic, Latin script	Not alphabetic, but logographic (using symbols to represent words, not syllables)	?
Written language	More formal, academic; different styles for different purposes	Similar to those of English	

* Features of languages and possible problems are based on general descriptions and ignore exceptional details. See Table 6.1 for fuller descriptions of columns 1 and 2.

Table 6.5 French*

Language feature	English	French	Possible problem or error
Syllable structure, e.g., consonant clusters (c-c's) at starts or ends of words allowed? Consonant–vowel (c-v)? Dropping, eliding, silent letters?	Frequent consonant clusters can be at start and end of words (e.g., *str-, scr-, -lms*); has silent letters, elisions, e.g., *can't*	Frequent consonant clusters at starts of words; consonant clusters of two letters word-finally; a lot of silent letters and contractions	Because some verb endings like -*ent* are pronounced like schwas, E learners may leave such letter combinations unpronounced
Borrowing or influences from other languages	Germanic and Romance roots cause inconsistent spelling or pronunciation patterns, e.g., *rough* and *ruff*	Some identical spellings but pronunciation differences	Sing French pronunciation; difficulty with English words with similar spellings but different pronunciations, e.g., *cough, through*
Word formation complexity scale: simple–midway–complex, e.g., monosyllabic (simple) to multisyllabic, prefixes or suffixes (complex)	Midway: some grammatical markings, e.g., *walk, walk-s*; some new lexical items (e.g., *nation, national*)	Midway–complex: many grammatical markings that are unpronounced; complex word formation, e.g., *anti-constitutionellement*	Learners may phonologically underuse grammatical markings
Misleading word translations; "false friends"	E.g., in English, *actual* means *real*, but *current* in some other languages	Many; borrowed word may look or sound much the same but has a different, if related, meaning	Inaccurate meaning
Gendered words: Natural? Grammatical?	Natural, only on pronouns (e.g., *he, she*)	Grammatical gender, M and F	Misuse of gendered pronouns when referring to "neutral" objects. Some differences from E in use of gendered pronouns

Table 6.5 Continued

Language feature	English	French	Possible problem or error
Articles: where and when to use; consistency	Rules for definites, generics, indefinites, mass and count nouns but inconsistent	No bare nouns; all common nouns preceded by overt determiners	Over-use of overt determiners
Spatial relations: how expressed	Prepositions: choice depends on meaning intended with particular verb used	Similar to English	
Copula (connecting verb)?	Yes, be, e.g., I am good; I am hungry; I was hungry. Past, present, and future tenses	Similar to English; sometimes have phrase instead of be phrase	Possible be–have error, e.g., I have hunger
Auxiliary verbs?	Yes, some dialect variation	Use of either be or have to form past tense; no distinction between present perfect and simple past	Which auxiliary (be or have) to use; how to form present perfect tense, e.g., I have eaten vs. simple past, e.g., I ate. Possible over-use of present perfect
Verb particles?	Yes, e.g., turn off	No verb particles in French	Difficult to master verbs like put in, put out, put off, put up
Forming questions	Aux inversion, Q words, do, e.g., Are you going? What time is it? Do you want a drink?	Inversion between subjects and full lexical verbs as well as auxiliaries (e.g., Viens-tu ce soir au cinéma? Come-you this evening to the movies?) No do	Do omission; possible full verb inversion

Language feature	English	French	Possible problem or error
Commands and requests	Direct imperatives; indirect directives, e.g., *Can you . . ., Why don't you . . .*; very indirect requests, e.g., *It's noisy in the hall* (meaning *Close the door*)	Direct imperatives and indirect directives + very indirect requests	Rare misinterpretation of speaker intent; possible difficulty knowing how to answer (Y or N) to, e.g., *Would you mind closing the door?*
Scale of verb marking: none–some–many. Consistent?	Some, e.g., -*s*, -*ed*, -*ing*. Some irregularities, e.g., *went*	Many irregularities across verb stems and richer verbal markings	Difficulty memorizing English irregular verbs
Scale of noun marking: none–few–some–many. Consistent?	Some: case marking on pronouns, e.g., *I, me, they, them*; possessives, -*s*, plural –*s*. Some irregularities, e.g., *two deer*	Some on pronouns, e.g., the possessive is formed by prepositional phrase	Over-use of, e.g., *the house of John* instead of *John's house*
Subject–verb agreement	For singular and plural	For singular and plural	
Type and importance, and consistency of word order	SVO; fairly important and consistent	SVO	No difficulty except post-posed adjectives
Subject dropping allowed?	Not allowed; dummy *it*, e.g., *It's raining*	Not allowed; dummy *it*	
Formality scale: casual–mixed–formal language (e.g., forms of address and use of names); gendered or age-based styles?	Mixed, tending to casual: slang, everyday speech, academic language; no formal age- or gender-based styles	Formal with outsiders, slang with friends and family; age-based and class-based styles	May be more formal when speaking English

Table 6.5 Continued

Language feature	English	French	Possible problem or error
Indirect speech scale, amount of hedging: none–some–much	Much, e.g., *I think . . ., maybe*	Much	
Classroom talk	Participates, asks and answers questions, engages in discussions	Active participation expected	
Writing system	Alphabetic, Latin script	Latin script	
Written language	More formal, academic; different styles for different purposes	Very formal and academic. Different styles	Difficulty mastering the variety of writing registers

* Features of languages and possible problems are based on general descriptions and ignore exceptional details. See Table 6.1 for fuller descriptions of columns 1 and 2.

Table 6.6 Hmong*

Language feature	English	Hmong	Possible problem or error
Syllable structure, e.g., consonant clusters (c-c's) at starts or ends of words allowed? Consonant–vowel (c-v)? Dropping, eliding, silent letters?	Frequent consonant clusters can be at start and end of words (e.g., str-, scr-, -lms); has silent letters, elisions, e.g., can't	Both syllables and words (most words contain only one syllable) are CV(N); no final consonant possible other than an <-ng>. Initial consonant clusters are common	Dropping of syllable-final and word-final consonants. Perhaps dropping of initial s- in consonant clusters; despite many initial consonant clusters, no spl-, spr-, str-, etc.
Borrowing or influences from other languages	Germanic and Romance roots cause inconsistent spelling or pronunciation patterns, e.g., rough and ruff	Chinese and Lao are the two most important sources of borrowed vocabulary	
Word formation complexity scale: simple–midway–complex, e.g., monosyllabic (simple) to multisyllabic, prefixes or suffixes (complex)	Midway: some grammatical markings, e.g., walk, walk-s; some new lexical items (e.g., nation, national)	Simple: no marking of number on nouns; no marking of tense on verbs. New words are formed primarily by putting free words together into compounds	Failure to use -s on plural nouns and -ed on verbs (and failure to use irregular plural and past tense forms)
Misleading word translations; "false friends"	E.g., in English, actual means real, but current in some other languages	English and Hmong are combined usually via code switching	?
Gendered words: Natural? Grammatical?	Natural, only on pronouns (e.g., he, she)	No grammatical gender; one third-person pronoun for all three, he, she, it	Confusion between he, she, and it

Table 6.6 Continued

Language feature	English	Hmong	Possible problem or error
Articles: where and when to use; consistency	Rules for definites, generics, indefinites, mass and count nouns but inconsistent	Obligatory classifiers on nouns when they are counted, e.g., "one round-thing stone"	Use of articles
Spatial relations: how expressed	Prepositions: choice depends on meaning intended with particular verb used	Some words can be used as either verbs or prepositions, e.g., one word for *put/place* as a verb, and *to/toward* as a preposition	Preposition choice
Copula (connecting verb)?	Yes, *be*, e.g., *I am good; I am hungry; I was hungry*. Past, present, and future tenses	Used with nouns ("I am Hmong"), but not with adjectives ("I tired")	Use of the copula + adjective construction
Auxiliary verbs?	Yes, some dialect variation	Yes, but they do not always appear before the verb	Word order in the verb phrase
Verb particles?	Yes, e.g., *turn off*	No, but some verbs are followed by other particle-like verbs	Verb–particle combinations must be learned one by one
Forming questions	Aux inversion, Q words, *do*, e.g., *Are you going? What time is it? Do you want a drink?*	No inversion. Q words not at start of sentence	Inversion; *do* omission (a problem for both questions and negatives)
Commands and requests	Direct imperatives; indirect directives, e.g., *Can you …*; *Why don't you …*; very indirect requests, e.g., *It's noisy in the hall* (meaning *Close the door*)	Mostly direct imperatives	Indirect directives and requests may be difficult to understand

Language feature	English	Hmong	Possible problem or error
Scale of verb marking: none–some–many. Consistent?	Some, e.g., -s, -ed, -ing. Some irregularities, e.g., went	None	Verb marking
Scale of noun marking: none–few–some–many. Consistent?	Some: case marking on pronouns, e.g., I, me, they, them; possessives, -s, plural –s. Some irregularities, e.g., two deer	None on nouns. Pronouns differ in number (including dual number) and person	Noun marking
Subject–verb agreement	For singular and plural	No subject–verb agreement	Subject–verb agreement
Type and importance, and consistency of word order	SVO; fairly important and consistent	SVO; fairly consistent	Differences in focus may impact word order
Subject dropping allowed?	Not allowed; dummy it, e.g., It's raining	Same as English, including dummy it	
Formality scale: casual–mixed–formal language (e.g., forms of address and use of names); gendered or age-based styles?	Mixed, tending to casual: slang, everyday speech, academic language; no formal age- or gender-based styles	Formality differences not as pronounced; use of complex language in speeches, sermons, poems, etc.; is not the same as academic language	Problems with formal, academic language
Indirect speech scale, amount of hedging: none–some–much	Much, e.g., I think . . ., maybe	Some; use of I think, but more common: use of discourse particles to "soften" a sentence, or convey speaker's attitude or degree of certainty	

Table 6.6 Continued

Language feature	English	Hmong	Possible problem or error
Classroom talk	Participates, asks and answers questions, engages in discussions	Different politeness practices, e.g., thanking others less overtly and routinely	Adult students may be reticent in class; young students may be less so
Writing system	Alphabetic, Latin script	Alphabetic, Latin script (modern)	Rare literacy in Hmong; familiarity with Latin script possible. Some different sound–letter correspondences may cause problems, e.g., letters x and s represent the sounds [s] and [sh], respectively
Written language	More formal, academic; different styles for different purposes	A written language only since the 1950s, so no agreement on a formal/academic style	Most students need help learning the differences between informal and formal English

* Features of languages and possible problems are based on general descriptions and ignore exceptional details. See Table 6.1 for fuller descriptions of columns 1 and 2.

Table 6.7 Korean*

Language feature	English	Korean	Possible problem or error
Syllable structure, e.g., consonant clusters (c-c's) at starts or ends of words allowed? Consonant–vowel (c-v)? Dropping, eliding, silent letters?	Frequent consonant clusters can be at start and end of words (e.g., *str-, scr-, -lms*); has silent letters, elisions, e.g., *can't*	No clusters at all; pronunciation is relatively true to spelling; does not contrast *r* and *l*; no *f, v, th,* or *z*; vowel differences	Spelling and pronunciation problems
Borrowing or influences from other languages	Germanic and Romance roots cause inconsistent spelling or pronunciation patterns, e.g., *rough* and *ruff*	Some Chinese-originated vocabulary, but not with present-day Chinese	Spelling?
Word formation complexity scale: simple–midway-complex, e.g., monosyllabic (simple) to multisyllabic, prefixes or suffixes (complex)	Midway: some grammatical markings, e.g., *walk, walk, walk-s*; some new lexical items (e.g., *nation, national*)	Midway to complex: productive use of prefixes and suffixes. Verb conjugation is highly complex	
Misleading word translations; "false friends"	E.g., in English, *actual* means *real*, but current in some other languages	Lots of English borrowing, but pronunciation, word formation, and/or meanings can differ	Vocabulary problems, e.g., *Notebook computer* vs. *laptop, sharp (pencil)* for *mechanical pencil*
Gendered words: Natural? Grammatical?	Natural, only on pronouns (e.g., *he, she*)	Grammar does not distinguish gender	Choice of pronouns?

Table 6.7 Continued

Language feature	English	Korean	Possible problem or error
Articles: where and when to use; consistency	Rules for definites, generics, indefinites, mass and count nouns but inconsistent	No articles. Demonstratives but no discrimination of mass count or singular–plural	Misuse of articles, possible over-use of -s with mass nouns
Spatial relations: how expressed	Prepositions: choice depends on meaning intended with particular verb used	No prepositions. Spatial relations often lexically encoded in verb itself (e.g., different verbs for *putting on a hat*, *putting on gloves*, or *putting something on a table*)	Difficulty with correct preposition choice
Copula (connecting verb)?	Yes, *be*, e.g., *I am good*; *I am hungry*; *I was hungry*. Past, present, and future tenses	Linking verb with nouns but not with adjectives (e.g., *he good*)	Some misuse of copula
Auxiliary verbs?	Yes, some dialect variation	Yes, auxiliary verbs are used to indicate tense and aspect of verbs	Possible confusion between *do*, *be*, or *have*, especially in negatives or questions
Verb particles?	Yes, e.g., *turn off*	Complex system of post-noun particles, marking grammatical functions; no verb particles at all	Difficulty with the differences between verb particle *off*, adverbial *off*, and preposition *off*
Forming questions	Aux inversion, Q words, *do*, e.g., *Are you going? What time is it? Do you want a drink?*	Q word but no inversion, no do-support	Incorrect auxiliary choice instead of *do*, e.g., *What are you want? Over-use of inversion in indirect questions, e.g., I don't know what should I do*

Language feature	English	Korean	Possible problem or error
Commands and requests	Direct imperatives; indirect directives, e.g., *Can you . . .*, *Why don't you . . .*; very indirect requests, e.g., *It's noisy in the hall* (meaning *Close the door*)	Similar to English	
Scale of verb marking: none–some–many. Consistent?	Some, e.g., -s, -ed, -ing. Some irregularities, e.g., *went*	Complex verb marking system with many uses, but no number marking	Difficulty with plurals, third-person singular -s, and irregular past tenses
Scale of noun marking: none–few–some–many. Consistent?	Some: case marking on pronouns, e.g., *I, me, they, them*; possessives, -s, plural –s. Some irregularities, e.g., *two deer*	Post-noun particles serve grammatical functions, are not considered suffixes	
Subject–verb agreement	For singular and plural	No agreement based on number or gender; less strict agreement as a part of honorific system	Omission of third-person singular -s
Type and importance, and consistency of word order	SVO; fairly important and consistent	SOV; relatively free. Also, no relative pronouns designating clausal structure	Overly free word order? Wrong relative pronoun choice
Subject dropping allowed?	Not allowed; dummy *it*, e.g., *It's raining*	Yes. Everything can be dropped if it is semantically not important (e.g., *What time? Ate dinner?*)	Use of longer subject rather than dummy *it* (e.g., *To finish every homework in time is difficult*); subject dropping rarer

Table 6.7 Continued

Language feature	English	Korean	Possible problem or error
Formality scale: casual–mixed–formal language (e.g., forms of address and use of names); gendered or age-based styles?	Mixed, tending to casual: slang, everyday speech, academic language; no formal age- or gender-based styles	Highly developed age-based honorific system; younger people do not address someone older than themselves by name	Reluctance to use names for teacher or senior; Koreans think English is a "less polite language"; they may not distinguish between formal and casual speech
Indirect speech scale, amount of hedging: none–some–much	Much, e.g., *I think . . ., maybe*	Much, even more than English. Indirectness often means politeness	Frequent use of "I don't know," "I'm not sure," or "I don't know well" to hedge, even when knowing the answer
Classroom talk	Participates, asks and answers questions, engages in discussions	In most cases, teachers talk, and students listen and take notes	Reluctance to ask questions; may consider it rude to interrupt teacher to ask a question
Writing system	Alphabetic, Latin script	Hangeul (Korean alphabet, which is relatively true to pronunciation)	Unfamiliarity with cursive
Written language	More formal, academic; different styles for different purposes	Most students literate in Korean, possibly some English as well	

* Features of languages and possible problems are based on general descriptions and ignore exceptional details. See Table 6.1 for fuller descriptions of columns 1 and 2.

Table 6.8 Russian*

Language feature	English	Russian	Possible problem or error
Syllable structure, e.g., consonant clusters (c-c's) at starts or ends of words allowed? Consonant–vowel (c–v)? Dropping, eliding, silent letters?	Frequent consonant clusters can be at start and end of words (e.g., str, scr, -lms); has silent letters, elisions, e.g., can't	Frequent consonant clusters as in English but more complex; spelling represents pronunciation more faithfully; some English sounds are absent	Pronunciation and spelling; certain vowels not distinguished in Russian (e.g., beat and bit) are in English; problems pronouncing th-sounds
Borrowing or influences from other languages	Germanic and Romance roots cause inconsistent spelling or pronunciation patterns, e.g., rough and ruff	Borrowings are typically transliterated into Russian according to Russian phonological rules	Variable English spellings of borrowed words
Word formation complexity scale: simple–midway–complex, e.g., monosyllabic (simple) to multisyllabic, prefixes or suffixes (complex)	Midway: some grammatical markings, e.g., walk, walk-s; some new lexical items (e.g., nation, national)	Complex: multiple suffixes and prefixes, as in po-na-pis-a-l-i-s'; extensive grammatical markings and new lexical items	Possible under-marking in English because it is rarer and less consistent than Russian
Misleading word translations; "false friends"	E.g., in English, actual means real, but current in some other languages	Borrowed word may look or sound much the same but has a different (often related) meaning	Incorrect meaning, e.g., in Spanish and Russian, the similar-looking word actual means current
Gendered words: Natural! Grammatical!	Natural, only on pronouns (e.g., he, she)	Grammatical gender (three-way system); partially based on natural gender	Over-use of gendered pronouns (he, she) for non-human referents

Table 6.8 Continued

Language feature	English	Russian	Possible problem or error
Articles: where and when to use; consistency	Rules for definites, generics, indefinites, mass and count nouns but inconsistent	No articles at all (either definite or indefinite)	Under-use and incorrect use
Spatial relations: how expressed	Prepositions: choice depends on meaning intended with particular verb used	Meanings can differ from English	Wrong word choice
Copula (connecting verb)?	Yes, be, e.g., I am good; I am hungry; I was hungry. Past, present, and future tenses	Copula used in past and future tense only; almost no use of copula in present tense	Under-use of copula in present tense (e.g., He good; or To me brother for I have a brother; or To me cold)
Auxiliary verbs?	Yes, some dialect variation	Be used for future tense (like would in English)	Misuse and absence of auxiliary verbs
Verb particles?	Yes, e.g., turn off	Prefixes (related to spatial prepositions) are used	Wrong particle choice; preference for, e.g., descend over go down
Forming questions	Aux inversion, Q words, do, e.g., Are you going? What time is it? Do you want a drink?	No inversion or do-support; Q words; also a Q word to form yes/no questions (optionally used)	Use of Q word but no inversion; do omission; intonation only
Commands and requests	Direct imperatives; indirect directives, e.g., Can you ..., Why don't you ..; very indirect requests, e.g., It's noisy in the hall (meaning Close the door)	Same as English	Misinterpretation of speaker intent is rare

Language feature	English	Russian	Possible problem or error
Scale of verb marking: none–some–many. Consistent?	Some, e.g., -s, -ed, -ing. Some irregularities, e.g., went	Many. Many irregularities	Incorrect use of irregular English forms
Scale of noun marking: none–few–some–many. Consistent?	Some: case marking on pronouns, e.g., I, me, they, them; possessives, -s, plural —s. Some irregularities, e.g., two deer	Many; fairly consistent, taking into account that various patterns are regular	
Subject–verb agreement	For singular and plural	For person and number in present and future tense; for gender and number in past tense	Possibly dropping agreement if seeking consistency for English
Type and importance, and consistency of word order	SVO; fairly important and consistent	Basically SVO, but much freer than in English. Important. Word order is governed by pragmatic rules (what's important, what's been already mentioned, etc.) and to express definiteness	Over-use of non-SVO orders
Subject dropping allowed?	Not allowed; dummy it, e.g., It's raining	Allowed in some limited circumstances. No dummy pronouns	Over-use of subject dropping
Formality scale: casual–mixed–formal language (e.g., forms of address and use of names); gendered or age-based styles?	Mixed, tending to casual: slang, everyday speech, academic language; no formal age- or gender-based styles	Mixed: slang, everyday speech, academic language. No formal age- or gender-based styles. Complex system of expressing formality through pronouns, names, and form of address.	

Table 6.8 Continued

Language feature	English	Russian	Possible problem or error
Indirect speech scale, amount of hedging: none–some–much	Much, e.g., *I think . . ., maybe*	Some	
Classroom talk	Participates, asks and answers questions, engages in discussions	?	?
Writing system	Alphabetic, Latin script	Alphabetic. Cyrillic script	Possible mistakes with letters that look similar but are pronounced differently
Written language	More formal, academic; different styles for different purposes	More formal, academic; different styles for different purposes; frequent use of passives	Possible over-use of passives

* Features of languages and possible problems are based on general descriptions and ignore exceptional details. See Table 6.1 for fuller descriptions of columns 1 and 2.

Table 6.9 Spanish*

Language feature	English	Spanish	Possible problem or error
Syllable structure, e.g., consonant clusters (c-c's) at starts or ends of words allowed? Consonant–vowel (c-v)? Dropping, eliding, silent letters?	Frequent consonant clusters can be at start and end of words (e.g., str-, scr-, -lms); has silent letters, elisions, e.g., can't	Prohibition of word-initial clusters of /s/ + consonant; reduced number of permissible syllable and word-final consonants and consonant clusters	Possibility of transfer to English of Spanish pronunciation habits, especially at outset of learning process, e.g., I espeak eSpanish
Borrowing or influences from other languages	Germanic and Romance roots cause inconsistent spelling or pronunciation patterns, e.g., rough and ruff	Not applicable to Spanish. Foreign roots are accommodated to fairly consistent Spanish spelling practices	Possible spelling issues if the root in question appears with different spellings in English and Spanish
Word formation complexity scale: simple–midway–complex, e.g., monosyllabic (simple) to multisyllabic, prefixes or suffixes (complex)	Midway: some grammatical markings, e.g., walk, walk-s; some new lexical items (e.g., nation, national)	Complex. Much richer inflectional verbal morphology, and far greater use of suffixal derivational morphology, often for affective purposes, e.g., diminutives	Possible overuse
Misleading word translations; "false friends"	E.g., in English, actual means real, but current in some other languages	Borrowed word may look or sound much the same but has a different (often related) meaning	Incorrect meaning, e.g., in Spanish and Russian, the similar-looking word actual means current
Gendered words: Natural? Grammatical?	Natural, only on pronouns (e.g., he, she)	All nouns carry grammatical gender (M or F) with obligatory gender agreement markings on accompanying determiners and adjectives	Use of he/him, she/her rather than it for inanimate nouns

Table 6.9 Continued

Language feature	English	Spanish	Possible problem or error
Articles: where and when to use; consistency	Rules for definites, generics, indefinites, mass and count nouns but inconsistent	Article is default determiner. Most nouns require prenominal determiner	Over-use of article
Spatial relations: how expressed	Prepositions: choice depends on meaning intended with particular verb used	Meanings can differ from English	Wrong word choice
Copula (connecting verb)?	Yes, be, e.g., I am good; I am hungry; I was hungry. Past, present, and future tenses	Two so-called copula verbs corresponding to English to be; tener (to have) sometimes used as equivalent of English to be	Some have/be confusion in cases where Spanish uses tener
Auxiliary verbs?	Yes, some dialect variation	One auxiliary verb in compound past tenses	Incorrect use of compound past rather than simple past. Semantic constraints of Spanish compound past different from English (also dialect differences in Spanish)
Verb particles?	Yes, e.g., turn off	No	?
Forming questions	Aux inversion, Q words, do, e.g., Are you going? What time is it? Do you want a drink?	Yes/no questions: inversion of word order or just intonation. Q words require main verb inversion; no do	Do omission; possible word order problems with questions like Does John smoke? or Is John eating?

Language feature	English	Spanish	Possible problem or error
Commands and requests	Direct imperatives; indirect directives, e.g., *Can you . . .*, *Why don't you . . .*; very indirect requests, e.g., *It's noisy in the hall* (meaning *Close the door*)	Mostly similar to English; differing verb markings for number and degree of formality/informality between interlocutors	Misinterpretation of speaker intent
Scale of verb marking: none–some–many. Consistent?	Some, e.g., -s, -ed, -ing. Some irregularities, e.g., *went*	All persons of verb have distinct person/number markings. Many frequent verbs have inconsistent verb stem alternations	Possible over-use of verb endings
Scale of noun marking: none–few–some–many. Consistent?	Some: case marking on pronouns, e.g., *I*, *me*, *they*, *them*; possessives, -s, plural –s. Some irregularities, e.g., *two deer*	Obligatory plural marking. In spoken language, plural suffix weakened or deleted in some common varieties	
Subject–verb agreement	For singular and plural	For singular and plural	
Type and importance, and consistency of word order	SVO; fairly important and consistent	Flexible. VS quite frequent with intransitive verbs. Object movable for topicalization	?
Subject dropping allowed?	Not allowed; dummy *it*, e.g., *It's raining*	Allowed and frequent	Subject pronoun dropping
Formality scale: casual–mixed–formal language (e.g., forms of address and use of names); gendered or age-based styles?	Mixed, tending to casual: slang, everyday speech, academic language; no formal age- or gender-based styles	Formality distinctions in second-person singular (universal); in plural (Spain only); pragmatics, often region-specific, are complicated	Possible problems in choosing appropriate use of first name vs. title + last name

Table 6.9 Continued

Language feature	English	Spanish	Possible problem or error
Indirect speech scale, amount of hedging: none—some—much	Much, e.g., I think . . ., maybe	Fair amount	
Classroom talk	Participates, asks and answers questions, engages in discussions	Possibly more passive	?
Writing system	Alphabetic, Latin script	Alphabetic, Latin script	
Written language	More formal, academic; different styles for different purposes	More formal, academic; different styles for different purposes	

* Features of languages and possible problems are based on general descriptions and ignore exceptional details. See Table 6.1 for fuller descriptions of columns 1 and 2.

Summary

This chapter focuses on a subset of languages that are among the most commonly represented in American public schools. Drawing on the experience and expertise of people who know at least one of these languages in addition to English, we offered comparisons between these languages and English. Ten linguistic consultants helped in the creation of the eight language comparison charts in this chapter. Whether native to English or to another language, all our consultants provided insights into the differences and similarities that could present challenges for speakers of these languages as they learn English. The consultants made suggestions for a useful list of comparison features that may be implicated in many of the common errors made by ELLs from one of these language backgrounds. Importantly, they explained their language's character-istics in the charts and made notations about possible problems. Teachers can use the charts after reading the background sections for interpreting them. The charts are intended as tools to help teachers identify the possible problems and their sources that ELLs with varied language experiences may have. Finally, we suggested that teachers develop ideas for solving the problems, try them out, and share the results with fellow teachers.

Discussion Questions

- What are some of the features of English that many ELLs from various backgrounds have difficulty with?
- Why might two students whose home language is Spanish differ in the kinds of mistakes they make in English?
- What is consistency in a language? Is English consistent?
- How can a teacher use the language comparison charts to assist the learning of ELLs?

Chapter 7

Creating Language-Savvy Lessons

This chapter provides some examples for teachers of different content areas and student ages that we have culled from various sources (e.g., teachers and colleagues). Here we show how language lessons can be incorporated into any content area and with any aged students so that ELLs can, with little effort, practice English language skills. We organize suggestions and examples for both primary and middle/secondary. We discuss 1) teaching language while teaching the basics; 2) engaging all children in language/culture lessons; and 3) continuing support of learning of Academic English—including reading, writing, and oral language across all content areas.

Teaching Language While Teaching Content: Discourse Scaffolds

We begin this section by reminding the reader that scaffolding is the adult complement to child bootstrapping (see Chapter 1). Taken together, they explain how growth can be produced. Here we expand on this conceptual framework to discuss *discourse scaffolds* and how to adapt lessons with the use of them so that students can learn both content and English.

Discourse scaffolds refer to the process of teacher–student communication. They involve 1) providing high levels of language support in the early stages of learning and 2) gradually taking the support away so that learners develop independence. Providing just the right amount of support allows student learners to take on more responsibility for their own learning.

Discourse scaffolds serve the purpose of facilitating learning, since the expert (the teacher) provides graduated assistance to the novice (the student) so he or she will learn. The most effective scaffolds provide support for students at the frontier of what they do know—their competence; this constitutes students' potential for new learning (zone of proximal development). Eventually, when no longer needed, the scaffold dissolves (Cazden, 1988).

Tharp (1994) reminds us that, "The critical form of assisting learners is through dialogue, through the questioning and sharing of ideas and knowledge that happens in instructional conversations. . . . to truly teach, one must converse; to converse is to teach" (p. 156). Eeds & Wells (1989) described the most beneficial situation for students' learning as one where teachers' scaffolds take the form of classroom discussions that are "grand conversations." However, they noted that, far too often in American classrooms, teacher–student instructional conversations more often are "gentle inquisitions." Types of scaffolds vary; they convey different expectations to students about their roles as listeners, speakers, readers, and writers; and this variation in turn influences the students' self-definitions (Wilkinson & Silliman, 2000). Harvey & Daniels' (2009) inquiry circles also are offered as a model for classroom conversations. Silliman *et al.* (2000) identified two types of scaffolds used in classrooms, *directive* and *supportive*. Each has its own structure of social interaction as patterned by the discourse of teaching. Each provides assistance to and possibilities for students' learning.

Directive Scaffolds

Wilkinson & Silliman (2000) emphasized that the directive scaffold is the most common in American classrooms. Teachers are the primary agents in transmitting knowledge and assessing students' learning. One particular type of the directive scaffold sequence is the most common in primary classrooms: the Initiation–Response–Evaluation – (IRE). This conversational sequence, exemplified by question–answer evaluation, is also the most well-known and studied of directive scaffolds (Wilkinson & Silliman, 2000). The consequences of using IRE sequences include 1) a passive orientation to learning, 2) an emphasis on the reproduction of information, and 3) assessment/evaluation as the responsibility of teachers.

There is a central role for the IRE sequence in classroom teaching, particularly if the evaluation element involves responsive follow-up and not just an opportunity for the teacher to assess the student's response. Positive follow-ups provide to *all* students the information that they can use for modifying their subsequent contributions (Tharp, 1994). As Gavelek & Raphael (1996) note,

> What matters greatly are the ways these different language opportunities connect among each other, the ways teachers mine these opportunities for their instructional potential, and the ways students come to understand that language is one of the most important tools of our culture.
>
> (p. 191)

Supportive Scaffolds

In contrast to directive scaffolds, supportive scaffolds much more easily allow integrating assessment with teaching. Support is given "on the spot" (Pressley & Woloshyn, 1995). This allows students to develop the capacity to understand, remember, and express perspectives in a greater variety of ways using both oral and written language, which is a key school skill. Gradually, teachers transfer responsibility to students over time to plan, choose strategies, monitor success, self-correct, and evaluate outcomes (Silliman & Wilkinson, 2007). This process is *self-regulation* (Brown & Campione, 1994; Brown & Palincsar, 1987). Self-regulation goes beyond students' mastering strategies. The essential element is for a student to know when and where particular strategies should be used (Bransford, Brown, & Cocking, 1999). Both supportive and directive scaffolds— indeed, all instructional practices—should take place in culturally meaningful experiences for students that help them to transfer what they have learned in the classroom to non-school settings (Bransford, Brown, & Cocking, 1999).

In classrooms, teachers can best facilitate students' learning by using *both* directive and supportive scaffolds appropriately. Stone (1998) envisioned sequences of scaffolds as cycles of communication challenges and inferences that provide a solution path for all students to understand the teacher's perspective. Teachers present students with a challenge (new information), discuss the information, and then adjust the level of assistance provided to the students.

Teachers decide which kind of sequence (supportive or directive) is most appropriate and effective for their English Language Learner (ELL) students in each learning context. For the sequences to be successful with ELL students who are learning both language and content, students must learn how to take the teacher's perspective on scaffold use in lessons. This allows both teacher and student to cooperate in using such sequences to enhance learning.

Table 7.1 summarizes the key points of the discussion on scaffold sequences by providing definitions and examples of some of the most useful and common classroom scaffolding sequences, *Modeling*, *Explaining*, *Participating*, and *Clarifying*. For each sequence, there is both a supportive version and a directive version.

Engaging All Students in Language Lessons

It is imperative for teachers to engage all students, especially those from diverse language/cultural backgrounds, in classroom learning processes such as scaffolding sequences. A central goal is to devise an *additive* language-learning environment. This type of language-learning context in school honors and enhances ELLs' home language and experiences as resources that can both enrich the classroom/school community and support the students' Academic English language acquisition (Danzak, Wilkinson, & Silliman, 2012). Classrooms that are characterized as *additive* stand in contrast to what Valenzuela (1999) referred to as *subtractive schooling*. From a subtractive language-learning per-spective, ELLs' home language and culture are perceived as "difficulties," or "problems," that must be overcome. This perspective aligns with a deficit model and ignores the *funds of knowledge* perspective in which culturally/linguistically diverse students bring both high worth and key values to the schooling context.

Culturally and linguistically diverse students who have the experience, knowledge, and resources to acquire academic language proficiency early on are more likely to identify with the cultural practices of schooling (i.e., reading

Table 7.1 Types of Directive and Supportive Scaffolds

Type	Nature	Definition	Example
Modeling	Supportive	Externalized schemas designed to "work through" a specific problem-solving strategy in explicit ways; often includes reasons for strategy selection and specifying the strategy's steps (Englert, et al., 1994; Roehler & Cantlon, 1997)	*Think-alouds*: Teacher verbally demonstrates thinking processes supporting consecutive steps in a task (Roehler & Cantlon, 1997). e.g., "Hmm. Two of the words I see in the sentence are words. I just know. However, that long one isn't one I just know, so I will just have to decode it. . . . I will look at each letter from the beginning to the end and see if there are chunks that I know. . . . Anyone have an idea how many chunks I should divide this word into to figure it out?" (Gaskins, et al., 1997, p. 56)
	Directive	The teacher engages in direct teaching of the concept or skill that is the focus of misunderstanding (Englert, et al., 1994); may involve either 1) "telling" the child directly what content to think about without further information on how to resolve the problem (Hogan & Pressley, 1997), or 2) providing indirect cues, such as phonemic prompts, as a method to retrieve content presumed to exist	1) Telling: "Look over here. You have your /g/ sound. Now you do vowel /go/" (teacher gives the initial consonant–vowel structure for "gold"). 2) Content retrieval: "That's not a /d/. Flip it over and it's a . . .?"

Type	Nature	Definition	Example
Explaining	Supportive	An explicit statement attuned to the child's emerging understanding about the concept being learned (propositional knowledge), why and when the concept can be used (conditional or situational knowledge), and how the concept should be used (procedural knowledge) (Roehler & Cantlon, 1997, p. 17)	"You've told me a lot about how to decode this word. You told me to break it into manageable chunks, and you told me how many chunks make up the word based on the number of vowel sounds. . . . Finally you were flexible and suggested several ways to pronounce the word" (Gaskins, et al., 1997, p. 58)
	Directive	Explanations may not semantically integrate propositional, situational, and procedural knowledge; students may be directed to attend to only one source of knowledge as the justification for understanding the concept	"A 'u' looks like a cup. Like this [holds up the letter] to hold water. . . . like a little scoop. And that's the lower case 'u.'"
Participating	Supportive	Teacher invitations to participate (Goldenberg & Patthey-Chavez, 1995; Roehler & Cantlon, 1997): 1) provide opportunities for students to contribute parts of the task that they may know and understand, 2) elicit students' reasons to support a statement or position, and 3) create opportunities for more complex language production through invitations to expand	1) Contribute: "That's a possibility, it could be TRANS LUH CENT. Are there other possibilities?" (Gaskins et al., 1997, pp. 57–58). 2) Reasons: "What makes you think that?" "How do you know?" (Goldenberg & Patthey-Chavez, 1995, p. 61). 3) More complex language use—"Tell us more about that." "What do you mean?" (Goldenberg & Patthey-Chavez, 1995, p. 61)
	Directive	Participation typically solicited by IRE sequences and generally limited to giving the correct answer to teacher questions; student language use is usually confined to single words or short phrases	Teacher: "What's your first sound?" Student: "/d/." Teacher: "That's not a /d/. Flip it over and it's a . . .? Student: "Bee" (says letter name). Teacher: "Good. Remember that's a letter on our word wall."

Table 7.1 Types of Directive and Supportive Scaffolds

Type	Nature	Definition	Example
Clarifying	Supportive	Teacher is responsive to, rather than evaluative about, whether student's emerging understanding is reasonable; if the contribution is not reasonable, then clarification is sought (Gaskins, et al., 1997; Roehler & Cantlon, 1997)	Student: "I know that when there is a vowel at the end of the chunk, the vowel says its own name—like in 'station'." [Student appears to be chunking "station."] Teacher: [Writes station on board with a space between the two syllables]. "What do the rest of you think? Any other ideas?" (Gaskins, et al., 1997, p. 57)
	Directive	Evaluation component of IRE sequence (E) conveys personal judgment about accuracy of the target response through either 1) positive evaluation, 2) negative evaluation, or 3) neutral evaluation (Silliman & Wilkinson, 1991, pp. 307–308); judgments may be direct or indirect	1) Positive: "Good, OK, great, that's a good way to do it." 2) Negative: "That's not quite right; You are close. Try it again." 3) Neutral: "Hmmm."

Source: Adapted from Silliman, E., Bahr, R., Beasman, J., & Wilkinson, L. C. (2000). Scaffolds for learning to read in an inclusion classroom. *Language, Speech, and Hearing Services in Schools, 31*, 265–279.

and writing instruction) and to meet the demands of school. Students who do not have this background most likely do not identify with those practices. One consequence is that they are less likely to engage in schooling and instruction (Danzak & Silliman, 2005). Without strong support to engage and develop their Academic English language proficiency, these students are at risk of disengaging, not learning, and "falling through the cracks."

As an example of the kind of support that may be needed, consider the Word Wall.

Word Walls

Word Walls are flexible and can be used for many teaching purposes in any classroom. Words can be continually added, changed weekly or monthly, and updated for special occasions or projects. Although there are a variety of Word Walls, typically for all of them, the words are large enough so that they can be seen throughout the classroom.

A key concept of a Word Wall is that it is interactive. All students should be able to reach the Word Wall to touch each word or to take the word off the wall. Word Walls can provide a learning environment that is richly concentrated with print, and thus provides opportunities for students to use the print in their literacy activities (Fisher, Frey, & Rothenberg, 2008). By seeing the words grouped by same letter or other spelling patterns such as consonant–vowel–consonant or silent *e*, students will begin to notice patterns and remember common spellings. If students are unsure of how to spell a word, they can use the Word Wall to check their spelling or help them with a word they are not familiar with. Thus, Word Walls offer students more independence and ways to interact with phonics, morphology, and vocabulary.

Although Word Walls can be beneficial to students, simply having one in the classroom is not sufficient. Students must be taught to use the Word Wall. They need to know some letters and sounds in order to be able to locate words. As with a dictionary, if students begin with the wrong sounds or letters, it may be difficult to find specific words. With the necessary appropriate preparation and instruction in their use, Word Walls can provide a highly motivating and interactive learning environment. Students can then use them to build their word and spelling knowledge, and to develop the reading and writing skills necessary to succeed in any content area. Word Walls can be used to display the specialized vocabulary of the sciences as well as the relations among words and concepts. Students using them will develop their skills more independently.

The following observation was provided by a classroom co-teacher, a graduate student of the second author. The example illustrates the use of Word Walls in a classroom enrolling ELLs.

In this combined grade 3–5, intermediate/advanced ESL classroom at an urban primary school, the majority of students had Spanish as their L1. The classroom was staffed by an ESL teacher and a co-teacher. The key vocabulary

Table 7.2 Example of a Word Wall

Words related to penguins		Words related to cacti	
Blubber	Regurgitate	Molecule	Erosion
Antarctica	Preening	Transpiration	Sediment
Insulation	Buoyancy	Expand	Dry head
Predator	Oil gland	Contract	Spines
Waddle		Survive	

words for thematic lessons were prominently displayed on the board and changed over the course of a month, depending on the topic they were covering at the time. For example, consider the Word Wall for two topics: penguins and cacti. (See Table 7.2.)

The classroom co-teacher said that she was amazed to see the complexity of some of the words listed by the regular teacher. She noted, "Since the majority of these words were not everyday words, but, rather, literate words and/or content-specific words, I wondered if the students should have some familiarity with them, or be able to define them. These vocabulary Word Walls were situated near 'hands-on' activities that were related to the topics of penguins and the cactus." The ESL teacher dedicated a great amount of time to vocabulary. She said, "I may only cover 30 percent of the book but I do it really well." Some of the activities included an introduction to a biology unit that generated curiosity among the students. For example, for the penguin topic, students first were asked to name the baby penguin in the zoo. The teacher focused on Humboldt penguins, which are native to the waters off the coast of Chile and Peru. Her students showed a preference for names with a connection to Latin America. The students researched the potential penguin names by exploring Spanish translations. The ESL teacher then encouraged and supported many activities with the students on the topic, such as reading from books and conducting in-class science experiments to demonstrate how an emulsion of oil and water simulates the ways penguins stay warm. Other activities included carrying an orange between their feet to duplicate the care and incubation of an egg by the father penguin.

The entry point for the study of the desert cacti was through the writing of pen–pal letters to ESL students in Arizona. Other "hands–on" activities included an experiment duplicating the waxy covering of a cactus to show how the cactus guards against transpiration (an example of a content-specific vocabulary word).

This example shows how Word Walls can be the fulcrum around which many activities are initiated. They can be useful for higher grades and all content subjects as well. For example, a math classroom might have Word Walls for key concepts, along with short, basic definitions. Teachers should keep in mind that the primary purpose of a Word Wall is to serve as a kind of scaffold, a topical, external framework to help students organize their learning. The creative use of Word Walls for all sorts of purposes is virtually unlimited.

Continuing Support for Mastery of Academic English

Students' school achievement depends upon their being proficient in the language of classroom instruction and textbooks. Participating fully in all classroom activities requires thinking and talking in ways that incorporate literate language and precise vocabulary. From elementary to high school, such skills are the *sine qua non* of success. For all students, developing full academic language proficiency takes at least a decade of schooling (Berman, 2007). In talking, reading, and writing, students must understand and easily use the vocabulary and grammar of the curriculum in subjects ranging from language arts to science to history and mathematics.

ELLs have the especially daunting task of learning academic language well enough to participate in all classroom activities even while they are learning English as a second language in school (Zwiers, 2004). The distinction between one's everyday oral language register and the more specialized register of academic language is a critical one, yet the distinction is not often noticed (Wilkinson & Silliman, 2010). For example, consider the following comments on ELL learning from a teacher who was enrolled in an undergraduate class offered by a colleague of the second author.

> Although I taught elementary school for several years, I never realized the vast difference between these two registers. The expectation that students would comprehend and produce language with academic vocabulary was almost a given—it would happen naturally. This is, of course, not the case with ELLs and students with speech/language impairments.
>
> (R. Danzak, personal communication,
> November 8, 2008)

Table 7.3 provides an overview of the contrast and continuum between "everyday" conversational oral language and the academic language used in the classroom.

In contrast to the oral language register that toddlers learn and children and adults use in everyday life, the academic language register represents a new tool for thinking and communicating in more literate ways. Teachers and researchers often misunderstand it to be limited to the use of content area vocabulary, for example, *revolution, satire,* and *equation* (Zwiers, 2008). However, much more than vocabulary distinguishes it from everyday language. For example, there is a major difference between producing words in natural conversation and the metalinguistic ability to talk about word units, such as "What is the root word

Table 7.3 Academic Language Register and Everyday Oral Language Register

Everyday oral language register	Academic language register
Vernacular discourse varieties that are more oral	Specialist discourse varieties that are more literate
Describes primary language abilities	Describes secondary language abilities and advanced literacy-related language abilities
Typical of face-to-face conversation	Typical of the discourse of schooling, including the discourse of textbooks and composition
Insufficient for academic achievement	Necessary for academic achievement

Source: Adapted from Wilkinson, L. & Silliman, E. (2012). Language. In J. Arthur & A. Peterson (Eds.). *The Routledge companion to education.* London: Routledge.

in *equation*?" Becoming a proficient metalinguistic user of one's language is intertwined with literacy learning and "continues across the lifespan" (Berman, 2007, p. 348).

The academic and everyday registers are related but independent (Cummins, 2000). This means that, although we can switch from one register to the other in a relatively seamless manner depending on the need and situation, we can still use each register separately. For example, in talking with close friends, we would likely use a relatively informal register whereas we would likely fully activate the academic language register in writing a research report on global warming (Wilkinson & Silliman, 2008). Developing academic language proficiency is similar in some respects to learning a second language. In their pre- and early schooling, normally developing children acquire a first language that allows them to become competent and cooperative conversationalists in their social interactions with family, peers, and others. Primary language learning results in persons knowing how to talk in the situations of everyday community life (Shatz, 1994). Academic language learning goes beyond this to produce a literate person, capable of communicating appropriately in a broader, more educated and varied world.

As an example of the way in which essential academic language vocabulary can be taught in an engaging manner, a general education teacher reported to two of our colleagues how she adapted the concept of vocabulary tiers for her own teaching of ELLs. Beck, McKeown, & Kucan (2003) had proposed the concept of vocabulary tiers, with the most basic vocabulary as a part of the everyday oral language register. Examples include words such as *flowers, baby, clock, walk, eyes, happy,* and *sad.* More complex words, including many associated with more literate academic use across content areas, are classified as Tier 2. Some examples are *mechanisms, attractions, predict, sinister, mention, detest, timid, absurd*, and *compose*. Many Tier 2 words are derivations; that is, they are root words to which prefixes and suffixes have been added. Finally, Tier 3 words are domain-specific words, such as *echolocation*, that make up the specialized vocabulary of a particular discipline. They are rarely part of everyday conversations and must be taught within the context of the discipline—in this case, biology. The following description exemplifies some of the ways that a primary school educator engaged her ELLs and non-ELLs in learning essential new vocabulary. This teacher was the student of the second author:

> I explained the concept of "academic language" as well as Tier 1, Tier 2, and Tier 3 words to my students. I told them that our goal is to use more Tier 2 words in our daily morning meeting, such as choosing the words from their theme assessments, as well as from the academic language we use on our state assessments. 1) I write the word on the board. 2) We say it. 3) I use it in context of several different sentences. 4) We make a "Tree Map" to list "What it is" (synonyms), "What it isn't" (antonyms), and "other forms" of the word. 5) Students try using the word in context. 6) I write one of their sentences with the word in context under the Tree Map. (I also use the term "context" when I want them to use the word in a sentence: "Who can use that word in context?" "Give me an example of that word in context.")
>
> The "fun" part is: THE CHALLENGE: teacher versus students. Who can correctly use the term in context throughout the day? Each time one of us used the word, we added a tally mark. For the word, "satisfaction" (*satisfy, satisfied, satisfying*), I used the word, or one of its forms, twenty-three times that day. My students used it forty-eight times! (I have to admit, sometimes they were a bit shaky in their usage, but if it was "passable" I let it go. The fact is, they were eagerly trying to use the word ALL DAY! We kept integrating previously used Words of the Day into our conversation, so when the time was right, I led them to understand the fine differences in their usage. Bit by bit, they truly started to use the words correctly.) The challenge lasted for the day, but, since we had the words on chart paper, we kept adding tally marks as they were used during the week.

Beck, McKeown, & Kucan (2003) also note that students do not always use the synonyms properly. The teacher describes the process that followed.

> For words with "semantic degrees," we started out with a "circle map" and just brainstormed all the ways to say "happy." Then I explained that words have very slight levels of meaning. I used a thermometer to explain the degrees or the intensity. As a group we tried ranking the words from least to most. I placed them alongside the thermometer as they were ranked by the class. I also used stair steps and placed each word on a step. While discussing the word *happy* (*glad, happy, cheerful, eager, thrilled, excited*), I also

gave them *elated* and *ecstatic*. Next, we went into the varying degrees of "rain" because we are working on a weather unit (*mist, drizzle, shower, rain, downpour*). I placed those alongside a thermometer and on stair steps. I asked them which they preferred to help them remember the degrees of intensity. They came to a consensus that the stairs were most helpful for remembering the words, but that it helped to use the thermometer to remember the intensity concept. (Remember, these are 95 percent ELLs!) So . . . we are now recording these words in our vocabulary notebooks on "stairs," highlighting the "Tier 2 and 3" words.

Examples of Language-Savvy Lessons in All Classes

Effectively teaching ELLs can be a challenge for both general education teachers and special education teachers. Often, solutions are not obvious. The following commentary was given by a special educator, who was a student of one of our colleagues. This special educator makes the cogent observation that educating ELLs is the responsibility of all teachers, not just ESL teachers. Her commentary provides a clear snapshot of teaching today. The commentary has an objective tone—not a rant, not exactly despair, just a clear picture of what she faces.

As a special education teacher, I've always looked at ELL strategies much like I have made accommodations for my students with learning disabilities and language impairments. I've tried to use a lot of visuals, rephrase, preview information, had the students summarize the lesson so that I know they understood it. I taught Pre-K Special Ed for five years, and I feel like these strategies were easier there. Maybe it was because most of my class was so language delayed they barely spoke or had so many other things going on, for example autism or behavior issues. Two years ago, I had a ninth-grade boy in my math class that had just moved to the area from Puerto Rico. On top of knowing no English, he had a learning disability that was diagnosed in Puerto Rico. We had an ELL assistant come to the room a few times a month to assist, but she didn't understand the math so it just made things more confusing. We used another student in the class that spoke Spanish to translate, but her math skills were also low which sometime complicated the issue. I tried to do a lot of modeling with him one-on-one, but it was very difficult and I don't feel that he received the services he needed. It was sad to see. We do have an ELL (actually called ESOL: English as a Second Language) teacher that provides services for two to three schools on a weekly basis. These teachers have very little contact with the students; they just maintain paperwork and assess. The classroom assistants are left to assist the students. Sometimes it's helpful, but sometimes they make it worse. It's difficult because they aren't in the class all the time to know what is expected, so how can they be asked to help? There is never more than one ESL assistant per school. So, in hopes, the classroom teacher has a "bag full of tricks" and strategies to use and is consistent. With the school's budget cuts, it's really difficult for everyone. And as far as special education, I think we will eventually serve as a resource more than providing direct services, much like the ESL teacher. It all will fall on the general education teacher.

(R. Danzak, personal communication, August 1, 2010)

General educators can equip themselves sufficiently so that their lessons are maximally effective for all students, including ELLs. Brisk (2010) reminds us that the essential elements for meeting this challenge are 1) creating a classroom climate and organization for optimal language development, and 2) integrating language with curriculum and instruction. With regard to the former, teachers can find ways to recognize their students' languages, culture, and talents, and utilize strategies that encourage participation from all students. Such strategies include 1) situated context lessons that draw on the background and interests of students, 2) thematic units, 3) non-linguistic ways of conveying meaning, 4) organizing students in a variety of groups, and 5) finding ways for students to apply their expertise to classroom lessons. Regarding the latter, general educators at all levels—primary, middle, high school—can embrace their roles as teachers of both content and literacy/language. Teaching language in context allows teachers to provide instruction in Academic English while respecting students' home languages.

In addition, Brisk recommends that all teachers should be teaching language "all the time and in explicit ways"; this includes discourse and text structure, vocabulary, grammar, spelling, and pronunciation. We have already noted how Word Walls and teacher–student challenges can be used in teaching vocabulary within any discipline and for any age group. Other aspects of language need only the creative preparation of the teacher to become part of a lesson. For example, Brisk reports on a second grade teacher who, in teaching history to her young students, included a discussion of how to talk about the past in English.

One tool that is particularly useful for general educators is our adaptation of Burns' Checklist (2011, personal communication), in Table 7.4, which is an easy-to-use scheme for checking to see if lessons meet the most basic requirements of being accessible to ELLs while simultaneously teaching content and English, particularly Academic English. Using this checklist, teachers can keep track of how well their lessons are planned to meet the needs of all students, especially ELLs.

Examples of Lessons Integrating English Instruction and Content

We offer some examples of lessons, one each from primary, middle, and high schools, which amply meet the three criteria set forth at the beginning of this

Table 7.4 Burns' Checklist for Adapting Lessons for Teaching Language and Content

My lesson plan has content objectives from science, math, and/or social studies	
My language objectives are based on language experiences during the lesson	
My language objectives include listening/speaking, reading/writing, language structures, and vocabulary	
All materials needed in the lesson are presented or described	
My Review/Assessment is tied directly to the content objectives	
My lesson shows different questions/responses for at least three levels of language proficiency in all four lesson presentation sections (Motivation, Presentation, Application, Review/Assessment)	
My home-fun activity (not homework) is based on one or more of the content objectives:	
Uses materials that are easily available in every home	
Is interesting to all members of the family	
Is do-able by the student if alone	
Results in some artifact to share in class the next day	

Source: Adapted from Burns, R. (2011). Personal communication. ESOL Lesson 1 Adaptation: University of South Florida Sarasota-Manatee College of Education Course TSL 4080.599 Syllabus (Fall 2010) Curriculum & Pedagogy of ESOL/Theory & Practice of Teaching English Language Learners.

chapter for "language savvy" lessons and exemplify Brisk's (2010) recommendations for 1) teaching language while teaching the basics—content and language, 2) engaging all children in language–culture lessons, and 3) continuing to support the learning of Academic English, including reading, writing, and oral language.

Primary Grade Lesson

The Very Hungry Caterpillar

This lesson plan offers a complete model of a lesson plan that has been adapted to include English learners at different levels of proficiency (AEL, 1998: *Help! They Don't Speak English: Starter Kit for Primary Teachers*). These goals are accomplished in multiple ways, such as the different kinds of questions (note the directive and supportive scaffolds) addressed to students with differing English language proficiencies. The questions focus on the same content but with different performance demands. The lesson can be used for students aged six to eight in both Grades 1 and 2—or beyond depending on the level of English proficiency of the students. This lesson may take two to three days to complete, depending on student responses and knowledge of English. While the complete and detailed description of the lesson is found in the primary source: *Help! They Don't Speak English: Starter Kit for Primary Teachers*, Table 7.5 provides the overview of both the content and language objectives for the lesson that can be used for Grades 1 and 2. Levels refer to levels of mastery of the language required to respond to the question or expression.

The materials required for the lesson include: 1) the book (*The Very Hungry Caterpillar*, by Eric Carle, 1987); 2) picture cards of the life cycle of a butterfly; 3) vocabulary pictures of foods, and word cards for days of the week, as well as markers, crayons, and glue. An optional element is use of a Word Wall for this lesson that can be posted in the area where the students will work on "hands-on" activities in connection with the readings. AEL (1998) recommends that, to motivate the students to engage fully in this extended, integrated lesson, teachers should take the following steps in sequence as the *Set-up Phase*.

1) Show students the cover of the book. Ask, "What is this?" If the students don't respond correctly, say, "This is a caterpillar." Tell them they will make caterpillars now.
2) Ask the students to make an accordion-fold caterpillar.
3) Ask the students to color the face. Show students how to accordion-fold the strip to make the caterpillar.
4) Paste the heads on the caterpillar bodies. Hold up your finished caterpillar and say, "Look at my caterpillar. Show me your caterpillar. Make your caterpillar move. How does the caterpillar move?" If the students don't know, say, "He crawls." (Point to the pictures and/or use other picture cards of foods.)

Table 7.5 The Integrated Primary Content Lesson: *The Very Hungry Caterpillar*—
Content and Language Objectives

Content objectives	Language instructional goals
Science	Identify common foods
	Recognize butterfly life stages
Social studies	State and sequence days of the week
Mathematics	Sequence using number 1–5
Art	Draw favorite foods
Critical thinking skills	Sequence butterfly stages of life
	Solve word puzzle
Language objectives	
Oral language: speaking and listening	Listen to a story
	Respond to oral commands
	Retell a story
	Choral repetition of story elements
Literacy: reading and writing	Dictate a similar story
	Read number words *one* to *five*
	Read and recognize the week days
Language structures	Recognize and respond appropriately to sequences such as: "Monday he ate, Tuesday he ate, etc."
	Recognize and respond appropriately to temporal sequences such as first, next, then, last
	Recognize and respond appropriately to question phrases such as "Did he . . .?"
	Recognize and respond appropriately to: "Yes he did. No he didn't."
Vocabulary	Review food words
	Know key words including: egg, caterpillar, cocoon, butterfly, first, next, then, last, ate, crawl

Source: Adapted from *Help! They don't speak English: Starter kit for primary teachers*. AEL Region IV Comprehensive Center, Arlington, VA., 1998.

The recommended *Detailed Presentation Elements* for this primary school lesson follow. Note that there are different levels of question complexity (as indicated by the numbers) tailored to levels of student language proficiency.

1) Show students the cover of *The Very Hungry Caterpillar*. Tell the students that this is a caterpillar; point to the word on the cover. Ask, "What do you know about the caterpillar? Where can you see a caterpillar?" Say, "Caterpillars come from eggs."

2) Show students a picture (from the picture cards) or model of an egg. Ask, "What is this?" (If students don't say, tell them, "This is an egg.") Ask Levels 1 and 2 (beginning), "Is something inside?" Ask Levels 3 and 4 (intermediate), "What is inside?"

3) Read the title of the book. Ask the students to predict what the story will be about. (Check to see if students know the word "hungry.")

4) Read the story *The Very Hungry Caterpillar*, while simultaneously showing students the pictures. When completed, ask students, "Did you guess the story? Were you right?"

5) Reread the story, encouraging students to join in chorally in the patterned parts. Use a cotton ball covered with spray to demonstrate what a cocoon looks and feels like.

6) Ask comprehension questions with "did." Elicit short answers with "did" and "didn't." Model if necessary: "Did he eat an apple? Did he eat a pencil? Did he eat pears?"
Level 1: nods yes or no.
Level 2: says, "Yes" or "No."
Levels 3 and 4: says, "Yes, he did" or "No, he didn't." Or a number.
Level 4: says, "Yes, he ate . . ." "How many did he eat?"

7) Focus on the past tense of "eat." Point to pictures and say, "What does the caterpillar eat? He eats plums. What did the caterpillar eat yesterday? Yesterday, he ate plums." Use the pattern with some other food items and ask the students to repeat and/or create their own similar sentences. "Did the caterpillar eat bananas? Pears? Strawberries?"
Level 1 and 2: nods; says, "Yes" or "No."
"What did the caterpillar eat?"
Level 3 and 4: says, "He ate bananas . . . pears . . . strawberries."
"Did the caterpillar grow big?"
Level 1: nods yes.
Level 2: says, "Yes."
"Why did the catepillar grow big?"
Level 3: says, "He ate."
Level 4: says, "He ate (a lot of) food."

8) Point to each picture in order and say, "First, it's an egg. Next, it's a caterpillar. Then, it's a cocoon. Last, it's a butterfly." Repeat this

procedure, having students point to each picture and repeat the sequence aloud.

Level 1: points to the response.

Level 2: repeats key vocabulary.

Level 3 and 4: repeats sentence.

Middle Grade Lesson

The Graphic Journeys Project

One of our colleagues, Robin Danzak, constructed and implemented a multimedia literacy unit, *Graphic Journeys*, in which thirty-two ELLs in grades 6–8 created graphic stories (comics) that expressed their families' immigration experiences (Danzak, 2011). The process involved reading graphic novels, journal-writing, interviewing family members, and integrating written text with family photos and other images to produce original graphic stories with computer software. *Graphic Journeys* had several purposes: engage all the students with a multi-literacies project; offer an authentic goal and purpose for writing; and unite all written texts under a common theme. The English as a Second Language (ESL) teacher and Danzak collaborated to facilitate the project in the English for Speakers of Other Languages (ESOL)–Language Arts classroom.

Throughout *Graphic Journeys*, ELL students had many opportunities to engage in authentic writing practices, thus providing ample opportunity for students to *bootstrap* their burgeoning writing skills. These activities, related to instructional strategies, included: 1) reflecting on the graphic novel, *American Born Chinese* (Yang, 2006), which was read aloud to the class; 2) composing short stories about their families, home countries, and immigration experiences; and 3) collaboratively editing each other's writing in an instructional context that highlighted various aspects of English syntax, spelling, and mechanics.

As students composed reflection pieces and family stories in their journals, examples from their writing were presented and edited daily by the class as an opening activity. Errors were used as "teachable moments" that were expanded to provide direct instruction on specific English language structures. For example, consider the error of a missing *-s* on a third-person singular, present-tense verb (a common pattern for ELLs and native speakers of various English dialects). The subsequent discussion highlighted the required use of this verb inflection and compared and contrasted this feature with other variations of the *s* morpheme, such as those occurring in plurals, possessives, and contractions. This approach stands in contrast to traditional grammar exercises, as the collaborative sentence-editing activity offered the students an authentic, communicative purpose for learning and practicing syntactic structures that would be incorporated in their graphic stories.

Along with the collaborative editing, the ELL teacher implemented several activities from the book, *Going Graphic: Comics at Work in the Multilingual Classroom* (Cary, 2004). For example, students were asked to write the dialogue for a series of "silent" comic frames, provide a title for an untitled work, enhance a comic with onomatopoeia, and draw pictures to illustrate a given, written dialogue. These activities allowed students to work with English vocabulary and structures in conjunction with the rich visual information provided by comics.

While students were exploring comics and graphic novels in the classroom and building English language skills through this process, they were also composing their families' immigration stories. Students interviewed parents and family members to learn more about these experiences, collected family photos, and wrote narratives in English. With the teacher's guidance, the students edited and revised their written narratives and, finally, integrated the text with photos and other visuals to create graphic stories of their immigration journeys. This was done with the support of Comic Life software (Plasq, http://plasq. com/products/comiclife/win).

The students' completed graphic stories were compiled and bound into full-color hardcover books that were formally presented to them at a large family event held at the school. Over 100 total students, parents, teachers, administrators, and community members attended this event, which celebrated the students' work and added yet another layer to the multiplicity of communicative modalities and meanings incorporated into the *Graphic Journeys* project. An excerpt from one of the written products for this project is presented in Figure 7.1.

The *Graphic Journeys* project can be adapted for any content area. For example, students could produce comics to summarize a novel (language arts), describe a natural process or cycle (science), recount a historical event (social studies), or illustrate a word problem (math). Projects like *Graphic Journeys* provide opportunities to discuss new concepts and learn how to express them in English. Additionally, graphic novels and adaptations have become popular and are now available in all subject areas. ELLs are attracted to graphic texts, not only for their visual appeal, but also because the illustrations support language comprehension.

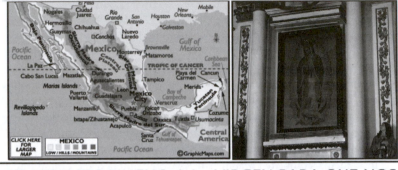

I was 2 years old when my father moved to the U.S. to work. He lived here for eight years off and on, coming back to Mexico once in a while.
When I was 11, my mom started packing up the house. I felt angry and nervous because we had a bad experience coming to the U.S. before. But this time was different.

LE PEDIMOS MUCHO A La VIRGEN PARA QUE NOS AYUDARA A PASAR LA FRONTERA.

Figure 7.1 Graphic Journeys Project

Source: Danzak, R. L. (2011). Defining identities through multiliteracies: ELL teens narrate their immigration experiences as graphic stories. *Journal of Adolescent and Adult Literacy,* 55(3), 187–196.

High School Lesson

The Immigration Project

The lesson plan described in Table 7.6 (Duquette, 2011) encompasses standards that influence student learning of both content (social studies, history, geography) and English language. The plan builds on the backgrounds of the students, as well as focusing on their knowledge to enhance the lesson for all students. The use of scaffolding techniques, including graphic organizers and charts, supports students in their understanding of the content of the lesson. Students are encouraged to participate by utilizing both directive and supportive scaffolding sequences. Several different forms of assessment allow on-going monitoring of students' comprehension and understanding.

Conclusions

We emphasize that teachers always should ensure that their students have access both to the language and to the content. Teachers should know what kinds of language demands their materials make on students. Specifically, they must be cognizant of the general English proficiency of the students and of any particular issues ELL students may have in identifying the language demands of each lesson. For example, any textbook or handout used will make specific language demands on students. Teachers should ask themselves, "How much of my explanation or assignment can *all* students understand?" They should be sure that a student has the necessary language processing skills and background knowledge—knowledge about the world—to understand, or the teachers should modify their materials. An important element for teaching ELLs is to build language and culturally relevant elements into lessons for all students whenever possible. Lessons should provide an additive language-learning environment that embraces ELLs' home language, culture, and experiences as resources to enrich the classroom as a whole.

Summary

This chapter has provided a framework and discussion of the goals for language-savvy lessons for ELL learners. We described two kinds of discourse scaffolding, directive and supportive, as ways for teachers to create conversations promoting language practice and learning among all students. We offered Word Walls and teacher–student challenges as two sample means of engaging students in the learning process. We discussed the importance of the academic language register for student success; we showed how it relates to everyday language and how the former builds on and goes beyond the latter. Finally, we provided examples of lessons for each of the three major school divisions that exemplify the goal of language-savvy lessons: to offer clear, engaging learning experiences for all students, including ELLs.

Table 7.6 High School Lesson on Immigration

Big idea/big question: What is immigration?	Key vocabulary: immigrants, immigration, destinations, persecution, native, refugee

Content objectives

Knowledge: Examine the reasons for which people immigrated to the United States and the kinds of immigration that existed, and how this relates to students and the prior knowledge that they have.

Process/skills: Students will identify what immigration is and draw upon prior knowledge to determine what they already know about immigration. Read/listen to the leveled reader; the students will identify the motivations people had for coming to the US. Students will draw upon resources to support their comprehension of immigration.

How assessed: First, students will be assessed through a pre-test that will evaluate their prior knowledge. Students will be assessed with their KWL performance, which they complete prior to reading [a KWL table, or KWL chart, is a graphic organizer designed to assist students' learning; the letters KWL are an acronym for "what we know," "what we want to know," and "what we learned"], and on their Cornell notes performance task, which they will fill out during the reading activity; this will be discussed subsequently. Students will be assessed continuously throughout the lesson on their comprehension and understanding of the content material.

Language objectives

Language awareness: Students will understand the leveled reader, and they will have an understanding of the content as well as having understandings and insights into the different kinds of immigration and how it connects to their lives. The students will be aware of the language use and the perspective used in the reader.

Language use: Students will develop academic oral language, listen to, read, and comprehend the leveled reader about the historical components of immigration. The students will use English to complete their Cornell notes, and they will use language in class discussions about immigration. Students will develop and use the suffixes *-ion* and *-ant*.

How assessed: Informal assessment of students' language use throughout the lesson will be employed, as well as assessment of their written language use with the Cornell notes.

Materials: Pre-test (Earle-Carlin & Hildebrand, 2000), KWL chart (Ogle, 1986), brainstorming webs (a type of graphic organizer), semantic maps (Chamot, 2009), suffix worksheet, *Immigration* leveled reader (www.readinga-z.com/), Cornell notes (Pauk, 2001), world map.

Table 7.6 Continued

Frame: access prior knowledge (preparation) Build Background Connect	1. Begin with the pre-test, to determine what students know before the lesson begins. 2. Use the brainstorming web: Each student will be given a web and the class will work together on this activity, brainstorming as a class what is immigration. 3. To activate students' prior knowledge, they will complete columns K and W of a KWL chart. 4. Semantic maps will be used to break down the word immigration and thus activate background knowledge to prepare for learning new information (Chamot, 2009). *Comprehensible input* ☐	*Check for understanding: review and assessment* Pre-tests will be used to determine prior knowledge; also the KWL chart will assess students' prior knowledge as well as what they have learned.
Support: deep processing differentiation (procedure, with time use indicated) Strategies Interaction Practice and Application Feedback	1. A short list of vocabulary will be pre-taught, which will include a mini-lesson on the suffixes *-ion* and *-ant*. Students should be aware of the function of prefixes and suffixes before reading the first two chapters of a leveled reader on immigration. 2. Write the base word *migrate* on the board. Students will be asked to explain what the word means or look up the meaning in the dictionary (e.g., "to move from place to place"). 3. Students will be asked to find two words on page 4 of the text in which *migrate* is the base word (e.g., *immigrants*, *immigration*). The teacher should state that both of these words start with the prefix *im-*. The teacher will ask the students to identify the suffixes that have been added (*-ant, -ion*). The teacher will tell the students the meaning of each (*-ant: one who, -ion: that act of*) and explain how the words are formed, for example, "*Immigration*: you have to change the word *migrate* to *migrat* by dropping the final e, adding the suffix *-ion*, and adding the prefix *im-*." 4. The teacher will discuss the meaning of *immigrant* (one who moves from place to place) and then discuss the meaning of *immigration* (that act of moving from place to place). Ask the students if these meanings make sense as the words are used in the book.	*Check for understanding: review and assessment* Students' comprehension of the suffixes through their suffix worksheet will be assessed; in these cases the students will add suffixes, and then construct meaningful sentences. Cornell notes will serve as an additional measure of student comprehension, assessing what the students understood in the text, and if they have focused on the most important aspects of the reading.

Table 7.6 Continued

	5. The teacher will write the words *assist* and *confide* on the board and ask the students to add the suffix *-ant* to make new words; the new meanings will then be discussed. 6. The teacher will write the words *act* and *direct* on the board. Next, ask the students to add the suffix *-ion* to make new words and then discuss their new meanings. 7. The students will then complete the suffixes worksheet. 8. The next element is reading the leveled reader, *The Story of Immigration.* This text was chosen to address students' individual literacy needs in the classroom by engaging them with text that is appropriate and accessible (Chamot, 2009). The leveled reader well conveys the main ideas that students must learn while at the same time using accessible language. 9. Students will be given Cornell notes, which support comprehension of the text. Visuals and maps supplement this section of the reading. *Comprehensible input* ☐	
Summarize: Evidence of learning Feedback Review and assessment	1. The lesson concludes by comparing refugees and immigrants, and connecting these ideas to the students themselves by asking about their own similar experiences. This discussion should include reference to adjectives that describe the feelings and difficulties that these two groups would have experienced. 2. This final activity will be an informal assessment of students' knowledge of adjectives prior to the mini-lesson on adjectives for the subsequent lesson. *Comprehensible input* ☐	*Check for understanding: review and assessment* Cornell suggests what needs to be re-taught, and what needs to be addressed, as well as teaching summarizing activities to promote reading comprehension. An informal assessment of students' knowledge of adjectives will be used, consisting of a mini-lesson on adjectives for the subsequent lesson.

Source: Duquette, T. (2011). The immigration project. Personal communication (June 17, 2011).

Discussion Questions

- What are some productive ways to address the oral language needs of ELLs in the classroom?
- How can teachers optimally support ELLs' building of English language speaking, reading, and writing skills in the classroom?
- How can we differentiate between conversational styles and the academic language used in classrooms?
- What are the unique challenges and opportunities that ELLs face in learning Academic English in contrast to everyday conversational language?
- How can we help ELLs learn content area academic language?
- How does academic language vary across content areas?

Chapter 8

Assessment

Adequate assessment of students' language/literacy skills should include an understanding of their use of language in all classrooms. In this chapter, we describe how assessment can be viewed as a way of collecting information about students when that information is closely related to the teachers' instructional practices and the learning environments that comprise students' school experience. We begin with a discussion of the two general categories of assessment, formal and informal.

Formal and Informal Assessments

Formal assessment utilizes a restricted selection of methods for obtaining information. There are specified guidelines for administration of tests, and the information collected is based upon and limited to their content. There is no supplementary information available, unless specifically noted, such as when the accommodations provided to English Language Learner (ELL) students are recorded. Formal assessments measure the knowledge that the student has learned in a specified time and are crucial for the student, as "high stakes"; significant, life-altering decisions will follow dependent upon the student's score on the test. The test results for a particular ELL student could be used to decide if the student exits services for English learning or if that student is placed in an advanced track for school learning. A second way in which formal assessments are considered to be "high stakes" is when test results are used for the purpose of school and, increasingly, teacher accountability. That is, the scores that the students obtain are purported to directly measure the success of the school and/or teacher's efficacy. Finally, "high stakes" testing can be used to screen students, as in the use of tests for student remediation, e.g., the testing for RTI (Response to Intervention) (Lipson & Wixson, 2010) where a student is to be identified for further instruction or services if these are necessary for him or her to make progress in school. Bailey (2008) reminds us that the technical qualities of a test, in terms of validity across similar students and test–retest reliability, are fundamental considerations, especially with ELL and/or immigrant students.

Informal assessment involves the collection of information in an informal but systematic manner. The use of formal assessment instruments (e.g., tests) needs to be supplemented by noticing, hearing, and seeing what students do with and by means of oral language across varied situations. Informal assessment allows tailoring the methods of assessment to the question(s) asked about students' language knowledge. This includes evaluative procedures that are developmentally and culturally appropriate for those students tested (Bailey, 2010).

Observations also can be made and used to evaluate the quality of the language environment of a classroom rather than individual students. The Sheltered Instruction Observation Protocol, SIOP, (Echevarria, Vogt, & Short, 2000) is one example of a commonly used observation protocol yielding potentially useful results for teachers.

We should, however, keep in mind that observation is more than looking at what is going on. Observation is a method of inquiry about students, the instructional practices in which they participate, the classrooms in which they learn, and the social situation within which teaching and learning take place (Silliman & Wilkinson, 1991). This can include a variety of methods, and it is continuous over a period of time, for example, the school year. This inquiry involves periodic collection of information via observation and recording of students' oral language to note changes in form, content, and/or use. Successfully applying these methods provides a more complete picture of each student's strengths, weaknesses, capacities, and language abilities. Common techniques can include the use of rating scales and checklists as discussed in Chapter 5, as well as qualitative methods including use of a running record and/or recording of key anecdotal evidence suggestive of trends and patterns.

For the purpose of both instruction and intervention, the use of standardized norm-referenced tests, as well as the classroom-based informal language assessments, are most commonly found in schools (Bailey, 2010). An example is when a teacher collects information about a sample of items within an aspect of language, such as vocabulary or sentence structure, and then determines how well a student is doing on these skills relative to other students at his or her age, grade, or level of overall language proficiency (e.g., the Language Assessment Scales, DeAvila & Duncan, 1991). The information garnered can also be "high stakes" for the student, since it can serve as the rationale to "sort" students into different ability groups such as reading levels. Bailey (2008) cautions us that the information garnered from standardized diagnostic assessment tools, however, may not be sufficiently refined nor contain a critical number of similar test items to allow identification of the needed specific sub-skills. William (2006) claims "The crucial feature is that evidence is evoked, interpreted in terms of learning needs, and used to make adjustments to better meet those learning needs" (p. 285).

Assessment tools for learning, including informal assessments, are an important instructional component for ELLs, since they capture a broad array of relevant information for teachers that is closely tied to ELLs' instructional needs. Teachers can use these informal assessments as part of "on the spot" instruction; these assessments may be designed in advance to address certain aspects of students' language knowledge such as vocabulary (e.g., Bailey, 2010). Bailey (2008) notes that the use of informal observations, for example, allows for a range of skills (e.g., student-to-student oral discourse) that are not always amenable to more formal or standardized assessment environments. Portfolios also provide opportunities for individual student profiles of language-learning progress and achievement, and thus are alternative methods suited to documenting ELLs' progress and facilitating teachers' decision-making regarding future maximally appropriate teaching and learning. A portfolio is a collection of information that has been accumulated about a learner's past experiences and accomplishments over a sustained period of time, such as a semester or school year. It is a useful tool for organizing a student's learning experiences and outcomes into a manageable form for assessment. Normally, a portfolio contains descriptions of learning with supporting documentation to explain and provide evidence of the student's learning.

In sum, direct observation of students' language and literacy in all classrooms is a key to understanding what is going on with the students—particularly those who are struggling academically as they simultaneously learn English and/or Academic English as second or even third languages. Informal methods of assessment can be based on direct observation in order to document students' typical day-to-day classroom interactions. Direct observation is a type of assessment that involves sampling information in an informal but still systematic manner. Careful observation can capture and clarify the school realities with which students struggle. These descriptions, in turn, can serve as the basis for teachers to make informed judgments about students' progress in the development of language and literacy skills across the curriculum and about their instructional effectiveness in promoting that development. It is a useful method for revealing what ELLs know and use of academic language in classrooms. Furthermore, observations can be used to clearly document any progress over time.

A key point is that content area teachers can assess content and assess language separately, so that a student who has very weak language skills may still be able to show a strong understanding of content. Both academic language and content need to be assessed/monitored continuously; separate assessments, at times, will be necessary to provide a complete picture of what a student knows and can do academically. For example, a student may have mastered a particular mathematical concept about fractions and be able to demonstrate that understanding using a tool such as Cuisenaire rods or graphic representations. However, this student may not be able to demonstrate that understanding through a verbal description or may not be able to recognize the understanding in a "word problem." Some teachers choose to grade ELLs with two grades: one for content and one for language expression/comprehension.

The importance for accurate assessment of directly observing how students and their teachers actually use language in classrooms should by now be clear.

The question is, "How should teachers do this?" The conceptual model outlined below can guide the use of observational methods for classroom assessments of students. This model provides a vehicle for sharing insights garnered from observations of students' language use in the classroom over time.

The Observational Lens Model

The Observational Lens Model (Silliman & Wilkinson, 1991) shown in Figure 8.1 is a conceptual model, a metaphor, for the particular approach to classroom observation presented here. Classroom observation is conceptualized as a series of snapshots that depict different views of events and behaviors of both students and teachers. This model may be useful to teachers as a way to organize classroom observations of ELLs and all students.

Like the filtering effect of the camera lens, human observers alter the reality of what they view. The lenses through which information is filtered are those cognitive mechanisms that allow interpretation of human actions relative to the contexts and purposes of interaction. Because different lenses filter information in different ways, only selected factors may be seen through the lens selected. The outcome is that any set of observational data represents a reduced version of the full picture. Observation is a method for revealing students' particular actions—what they actually say and do. Selection of the most appropriate lens for observing students' actions in the classroom depends on the purpose of the

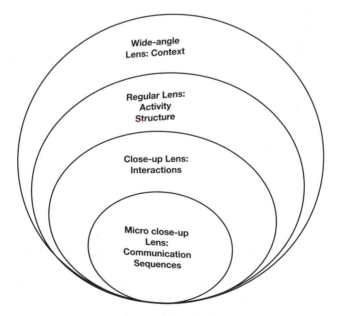

Figure 8.1 Observational Lens

observation. The lenses of the model offer four different perspectives, becoming increasingly more detailed and focused on particular aspects of classrooms and student learning.

The Wide-Angle Lens

The wide-angle observational lens is best suited to capturing an overview of learning across different classroom activities. The checklist in Table 5.4 and rating scale in Table 5.6, which are presented in Chapter 5, are examples of observational tools that yield a wide-angle perspective of a student's classroom learning. Burns' checklist for adapting lessons for ELLs, Table 7.4 (Checklist for Adapting Lessons), is a good example of general aspects of the lesson that teach both English language and particular subject-area content.

The Regular Lens

The regular lens provides a more detailed insight into how effectively a student understands the structure of a particular classroom activity such as the "read aloud" in reading groups. Table 5.5 (Expanded Checklist for Students' Oral Language) in Chapter 5 is an example of a more detailed description that provides the particulars about a student's performance.

The Close-Up Lens

The close-up lens permits a more detailed picture of patterns involving teachers and students engaged in a specific activity at a particular point in time. For example, a close-up view can illuminate critical actions that demonstrate a student's need for discourse scaffolding within a particular task, such as responding to wh- questions in the Initiation–Response–Evaluation (IRE) sequence, as discussed in Chapter 7 (see Table 7.1, which refers to specific information about questions, statements, etc. at the close-up level). An example of detailed analysis of these questions can be found in Wilkinson & Spinelli, 1983.

The Micro Close-Up Lens

If the purpose of the observation is to be at a granular level, then the micro close-up lens is used. At this most detailed level, this lens is used to reveal in fine detail the dynamics of interaction over time so as to address specific questions about a student's language and communication. An example would be whether an ELL with Spanish as a home language produces the sounds of *b* and *v* correctly and has come to understand that, while this phoneme distinction does not exist in the spoken Castilian dialect of Spanish. The distinction is a critical one for English in both speaking and writing. The tables in Chapter 6 offer examples of areas of potential language interference or difficulty by contrasting features of English with those of other languages. Using the tables in conjunction with micro-lens observation of a student's language behavior may aid the teacher to understand the basis of potential student problems.

Integrating Assessment and Instruction

Bailey (2010) has provided an example of the effective use of direct observation of a classroom in Los Angeles where assessment and instruction (both content and English language) are well integrated. Bailey summarizes the results of her observations at the Para Los Niños Charter Elementary School as part of a project designed to characterize academic language at the pre-kindergarten and kindergarten levels. The goal of this work was to help teachers build strategies that would facilitate the transition of young students across multiple school settings. The kindergarteners are Spanish-home-language students who have been receiving English language exposure and instruction through their mathematics and science classes. The following example is taken from a science lesson in which students, working in pairs, created trees to represent each of the four seasons. However, the design and key points can be transferred to other content areas. Bailey (2010) uses a variety of observational lenses as required by various purposes.

> Kindergarteners have been working on understanding the seasons of the year. On this day, the teacher sends children to work in pairs at various activities she has planned to construct trees representing the months of the year. The students immediately get to work. They are eager to make the trees! The children talk amongst each other excitedly, planning how they will make the tree and figuring out who will do what. The teacher comes by to check on the students' progress.
>
> (Bailey, 2010, p. 242)

Bailey's (2010) observation shows how both instruction and assessment for both science and the English language are seamlessly integrated. The strength of her example comes from her examining several aspects of the lesson, science concept-building exchanges, language-building exchanges, and formative assessment of both science and language knowledge. We summarize here Bailey's (2010) recounting of this classroom work; for a full explanation and details, the reader should consult Bailey (2010).

For science concept-building exchanges, Bailey's (2010) analysis shows that, by identifying differences between the students' class work, the teacher can scaffold a conversational exchange among students to emphasize the key aspects of the science concept under study. For example, the teacher can say, "José and Danny, I notice that the trees you made look very different! What seasons were each of you trying to represent? Why do the trees look so different?" "Alex, I notice that your winter tree looks very different from Lila's. Why is that?" (Bailey, 2010).

For language-building exchanges, Bailey's (2010) approach shows that, by talking with and listening to students, the teacher can facilitate the acquisition of language at the vocabulary, grammar, and discourse levels; these provide examples of the scaffolding technique discussed in Chapter 7. For vocabulary, questions such as, "What do we call that season?" give children opportunities to retrieve vocabulary in ways that are more cognitively demanding than questions in which the desired vocabulary item is supplied (e.g., "Is this tree in spring or summer?"). For grammar and discourse, open-ended prompts such as, "I'm so curious to hear about your work. Tell me about your tree", encourage children to respond with more than just one word. Open-ended prompts should lead to elaborated responses that can encourage dialogue among students as well as between student and teacher.

Bailey (2010) goes on to note that such an activity provides many opportunities for both the evaluation and support of students' learning by asking questions such as, "What season are you representing with this tree? What materials are you planning to use? Why?" One key component is that students should be asked why they have chosen particular materials and be able to explain the aspects of the season that warrant such selections. Such a conversation allows evaluation of both language and science learning.

We conclude this discussion of assessment by providing some examples in Table 8.1 of on-going, non-formal assessment tools that can easily be adapted for classrooms with a language or culturally diverse student body. In addition to the Language Comparison Charts described in Chapter 6, teachers may find some of the assessment techniques and tools in the table useful. We encourage their use with ELL and non-ELL students to determine their proficiency in content tasks themselves. They can gauge the English proficiency required of students to both understand the task demands and be able to reveal underlying content knowledge. We have also included formal unit tests and quizzes in Table 8.1, and, although not strictly considered to be on-going informal assessments, these tools are part of the repertoire for teachers as well. The examples in Table 8.1 are organized by the name, the time of administration (before, after, or during the lesson), a brief description, and a reference.

Summary

Adequate assessment of students' language/literacy skills should include an understanding of their use of language in all classrooms. In this chapter, we described how assessment can be viewed as a way of collecting information about students when that information is closely related to the teachers' instructional practices and the learning environments that comprise students' school experience. We discussed two general categories of assessment, formal and informal. An important point is that both academic language and content need to be assessed/monitored continuously; separate assessments will at times be necessary to provide a complete picture of what a student knows and can do

Table 8.1 Classroom Assessment Activities

Name	Timing	Description	Reference(s)
Checklist for content-specific language	Pre	ELL's content-specific language functions are assessed for: listening, speaking, reading, writing; three categories (not at all, some of the time, most of the time)	Hamayan & Perlman (1990)
Native-language literacy screening device	Pre	ELL student completes a questionnaire in their L1 along with writing a short story about his or her family	Hudson River Center (1999)
Do now	Pre	Assesses ELL knowledge of materials and language-use proficiency; teacher requires ELL students to do a short writing assignment in real time, no preparation, no editing	
Quick write	Pre	Assesses ELL knowledge of materials and language-use proficiency; ELL responds to a prompt (a question, a sentence starter or a statement). ELL has 3–5 minutes to compose a response and write it down; this response provides information about ELL's knowledge of the material and informal assessment of an ELL's writing (grammar, vocabulary, etc.); modification can include using culturally relevant materials	Fisher, Frey, & Rothenberg (2008)
KWL	Pre and post	ELL states what he or she knows about a topic, wants to know, and has learned; ELL students share the knowledge they have and that they wish to learn; post is what they say they have learned; important to consider cultural factors	Verplaetse & Migliacci (2008); Bailey (2008)
Student discussions	During	Teacher observes and records ELL student's discussions; informally assess oral language (clarity, fluency, content, prior knowledge)	Bailey (2010)
Initiation–Response–Evaluation (IRE) sequences	During	Assesses student's learning; teacher asks question that can be answered with a brief response which is evaluated by the teacher, thus providing feedback	Wilkinson & Spinelli (1983); Bailey (2010)

Name	Timing	Description	Reference(s)
Clipboard observations	During	Teacher writes down on a clipboard or post-it notes throughout class what he or she observes about the ELL student's progress, attitudes, habits, and social interaction to do with language	Faltis & Coulter (2008)
Think pair share	During	Students first think of their response to a question or prompt then share ideas with a partner; provides authentic interaction with peers to negotiate the materials; encourages students to use academic language; provides modeling from peers; teachers can monitor ELL language use in the classroom	Fisher, Frey, & Rothenberg (2008)
Exit tickets	Post	ELL student is required to list information he or she has learned as well as writing down any lingering questions	Verplaetse & Migliacci (2008)
Test/quizzes	During/post	To assess vocabulary, aspects of literacy, and/or content; makes ELL students accountable for their learning and encourage review of instruction from prior week; can be differentiated for level of home language for ELLs; important to include accommodations as needed	Bailey (2010)
Culminating project	Post	A culminating project-based assessment can be used with an individual ELL or in groups; can focus on writing; reveals what ELL has learned throughout the unit/year; use rubrics to score	Bailey (2010)
Portfolios	Post	Tracks ELL student's developmental progress and achievement throughout a unit or the entire year; consists of collection of student's work and information about the student that is helpful in interpreting the work; can be shared with parents and to other teachers to show ELL progress; develops meta-cognitive strategies	Bailey (2008)
Performance assessments	Post	Includes a project to reveal understanding in a variety of ways	Bailey (2010)
Survey	Pre	Home survey for ELL parents to complete; collect information about ELL's knowledge of home language and English	Bailey (2010)

academically. We concluded the chapter with a consideration of some examples of assessment tools that can easily be adapted for classrooms with a language or culturally diverse student body. We encourage their use with ELL and non-ELL students to determine their proficiency in the content tasks themselves as well as that required to both understand task demands and display their language knowledge.

Discussion Questions

* How should the assessment of ELLs be modified to reflect the language and cultural considerations of these students?
* Why is it important to use a variety of assessment tools?
* How can we tell whether a problem is language-related or content-related or both?
* What are some of the language errors of ELLs that may be mistakenly taken as evidence for language delay or disorder (see Chapter 6)?

Appendix A

Selected Web Sites

Professional Organizations

www.readwritethink.org

This web site was constructed by both the International Reading Association and the National Council for Teachers of English; it provides educators and students access to the highest-quality practices and resources in reading and language arts instruction. This includes professional development activities and standards-based lesson plans written and reviewed by educators using current research and the best instructional practices.

www.ncte.org

This web site is the home of the National Council of Teachers of English; there are many resources including lesson preparation materials for teachers.

www.nabe.org

This web site is the home of the National Association for Bilingual Education, and provides rich resources for English learners.

www.ncela.gwu.edu

This web site provides access to materials and resources about English learners, including the most current research findings; it is funded by the US Department of Education.

www.ncela.gwu.edu/content/30_innov

This web site provides an online monthly series, *Innovations for English Learners*, highlighting innovative practices from the field that show promise for advancing the education of English learners. The purpose of this series is for the community of English language educators to have a platform to exchange ideas and connect with other educators who have met similar challenges.

www.cal.org

This web site is the home for the Center for Applied Linguistics and provides rich resources about English learners, their teachers, and caregivers.

http://cecerdll.fpg.unc.edu

This web site is the home of the recently formed Center for Early Care and Education Research—Dual Language Learners at the University of North Carolina. Its research briefs give useful background on preschooler DLLs.

www.rae.es

This web site is the home of the Spanish Royal Academy. It provides much information about the Spanish language.

Examples

www.youtube.com/watch?v=wgWQoZz6nEk&feature=PlayList &p=5C4607319E0E1B57&index=0&playnext=1

This URL offers a video of a trilingual child, with the mother speaking only Indonesian, while the father speaks mainly French, with one sentence in English ("Okay, fix it then"); the child addresses the mother in Indonesian, the father and brother in French, with some English mixed in.

www.billingsmiddleschool.org/academics/designweek111/ overview

This web site provides a good example of a school that serves English learners.

www.byki.com/byki_descr.html

This web site provides resources to review vocabulary and phrases in a well-executed multimedia format including more than seventy languages.

www.colorincolorado.org

This web site provides a bilingual site for English learners, their families, and educators.

www.mamalisa.com/

This web site offers Mama Lisa's world of children and international culture, including children's songs, rhymes, and stories from around the world.

Tools

www.wordsift.com

This web site provides teachers with a tool for growing and enriching the academic vocabulary of their students (especially English learners) across the grade levels, and especially through academic content instruction.

http://en.childrenslibrary.org/

This web site for the International Children's Digital Library provides children's books in many languages; it is easy to search and use.

www.velazquezpress.com/Word-to-Word-Glossary

This web site offers a word-to-word glossary; however, it is of assistance only to those students who do know a concept in Spanish.

http://digitalis.nwp.org/resource/1226

This web site offers examples and guidance about how to encourage English Language Learners (ELLs) in their collaborative writing across the curriculum, using media tools such as blogs and digital stories.

www.wdl.org/en/

This web site provides key information on language origins, where the language is spoken, and what details about the language guide the spoken version.

www.rhinospike.com

This web site provides foreign-language audios on demand. You can submit a request for written text to be audio-recorded in the language of your choice.

http://languages.iloveindia.com/

This web site provides information on Indian languages (in English).

www.omniglot.com

This web site allows the user to "click" on languages (a–z) and discover a rich array of information about many languages. The first element of each language page provides the alphabetic information for each language. You can even hear how common words or phrases (like *hello*) in that language sound, and there are links to language lessons as well.

www.migrationinformation.org/ellinfo/FactSheet_ELL3.pdf

This file contains a great deal of information on the home languages of ELLs around the nation. It has a connecting link to details on the top languages state by state.

www.asha.org/practice/multicultural/Phono.htm

The American Speech-Language-Hearing Association (ASHA) provides phonemic inventories of several common home languages.

Suggestions for Further Reading

Listed here are books for readers who may want to delve further into the various topics presented in this book. The list has two parts. The first section relates to topics covered largely in Chapters 1–4, on language, language development, and bilingualism. The second part of the list more directly concerns the issues in Chapters 5–8, on teaching, learning, and assessment, particularly of English Language Learners (ELLs). We do not necessarily agree with everything presented in these books, but a few are classic, and all are well-written and present engaging, thoughtful arguments.

On Language and Development

Cook, V. & Bassetti, B. (Eds.) (2011). *Language and bilingual cognition*. London: Psychology Press.
   This volume provides chapters reviewing recent work on the relations between language and cognition, using evidence from bilinguals.

Cummins, J. & Early, M. (2011). *Identity texts: The collaborative creation of power in multilingual schools*. Stoke-on-Trent, UK: Trentham Books.
   This volume presents a unique approach to bilingual children's writing, by extending the narrative genre to the affirmation of language identity in the classroom.

Goffman, E. (1981). *Forms of talk*. Philadelphia: University of Pennsylvania Press.
   Erving Goffman was a well-known sociolinguist who was one of the pioneers of conversational analysis. Five of his essays on verbal interactions comprise this book.

Hoff, E. (2009). *Language development* (4th ed.). Belmont, CA: Wadsworth.
   This is an accessible, comprehensive text on language development, including sections on child bilingualism and language in the school years.

Lakoff, G. & Johnson, M. (1994). *Metaphors we live by.* Chicago: University of Chicago Press.
This classic book describes deep relations between language and thought, and may help teachers think about their language and the potential for misunderstandings among ELLs.

McCardle, P. & Hoff, E. (Eds.) (2006). *Childhood bilingualism.* Clevedon, UK: Multilingual Matters.
A product of a workshop held in 2004 in Washington, DC, this book reports on the state-of-the-art research in the field of bilingualism.

Pinker, S. (1994). *The language instinct: How the mind creates language.* New York: Harper Collins.
This classic book offers an engaging discussion of the human capacity for language.

Potowski, K. (2010). *Language diversity in the USA.* New York: Cambridge University Press.
This book reports on the twelve most common languages currently found in the US and discusses the problems of current-day immigrants in learning English.

Shatz, M. (1994). *A toddler's life: Becoming a person.* New York: Oxford University Press.
This book, written for the educated layperson, illustrates the bootstrapping model by describing the social, cognitive, and language development of a child from fifteen months to three years of age.

Verran, H. (2001). *Science and an African logic.* Chicago: University of Chicago Press.
Recommended by one of our language consultants, this book offers a glimpse into the logic and mathematical thinking of another culture and reveals how science is taught in that setting.

On Learning and Teaching

Calderón, M. (2007). *Teaching reading to English language learners: Grades 6–12.* Thousand Oaks, CA: Corwin.
For teaching reading, this volume is well-tested in the field of professional development and includes instructional activities to use with ELL students in sixth to twelfth grade classrooms.

Commins, N. L. & Miramontes, O. B. (2005). *Linguistic diversity and teaching.* Mahway, NJ: Erlbaum.

This book, reprinted in the Routledge series, Reflective Teaching and the Social Conditions of Schooling, includes four case studies recounting the kinds of difficulties teachers face when dealing with a diverse student body. The authors also report on the public arguments about language in the schools and offer suggestions on how all educators can work toward an education of high quality for all students.

Durgunoglu, A. & Goldenberg, C. (Eds.) (2011). *Dual language learners: The development and assessment of oral and written language.* New York: Guilford. This volume addresses ELLs' acquisition of the oral language and literacy skills necessary for school success. It includes guidelines for identifying students whose limited English may indicate underlying language impairment, as opposed to emerging language proficiency.

Garcia, O. & Kleifgen, J. (2010). *Educating emergent bilinguals: Policies, programs, and practices for English learners.* New York: Teachers College. This book is an accessible guide that incorporates current research findings to demonstrate how ignoring children's bilingualism perpetuates inequities in their schooling. It includes descriptions of alternative educational practices on students' home languages and literacy practices in schools, curricular and pedagogical innovations, and suggestions for enhancing both parental and community engagement.

Goldenberg, C. & Coleman, R. (2010). *Promoting academic achievement for English language learners.* Thousand Oaks, CA: Corwin. This volume provides a way to navigate the current research on promoting success among students who speak little or no English, and to discover specific recommendations for developing effective policies and programs.

Help! They don't speak English: A resource guide for educators of limited English proficient migrant students: Grades Pre-K-6 (1998, 3rd ed.). Arlington, VA: AEL. This volume provides an overview of best practices for English learners, as well as specific lessons and templates for use in primary school classrooms.

Lems, K., Miller, L., & Soro, T. (2010). *Teaching reading to English language learners: Insights from linguistics.* New York: Guilford. This volume skillfully weaves together key linguistic concepts with those related to reading (both theory and practice), including practical classroom-based suggestions for instruction and assessment.

Paradis, J., Genesee, F., & Crago, M. (2011). *Dual language development and disorders: A handbook on bilingualism and second language learning* (2nd ed.). Baltimore, MD: Brookes Publishers.

This volume describes bilingual language impairment from the perspective of typical development in dual language children. The authors emphasize cognitive, socio-cultural, and educational aspects of development in addition to the focus on language.

Shatz, M. & Wilkinson, L. C. (Eds.) (2010). *The education of English language learners: Research to practice.* New York: Guilford.
This volume presents evidence-based strategies for supporting English language learners by promoting meaningful communication and language use across the curriculum.

Soto-Hinman, I. & Hetzen, J. (2009). *The literacy gaps: Bridge building for English language learners and Standard English learners.* Thousand Oaks, CA: Corwin.
The authors provide strategies, examples, and tools to address the gap between ELLs and texts, socio-cultural differences between teachers and ELLs, and language differences between ELLs and peers.

Swan, M. & Smith, B. (Eds.) (2001). *Learner English* (2nd ed.). Cambridge, UK: Cambridge University Press.
This book offers extensive discussion of the characteristics of twelve common languages of ELLs and the kinds of problems they may cause.

Verplaetse, L. & Migliacci, N. (Eds.) (2008). *Inclusive pedagogy for English language learners: A handbook of research-informed practices.* New York: Lawrence Erlbaum Associates, Taylor & Francis Group.
This volume offers an overview of teaching practices that address the challenges and unique strengths presented by ELLs. The succinct and accessible descriptions of practices and strategies devised to improve the teaching of ELLs at every grade level are replicable in mainstream classrooms.

Wilkinson, L. C., Morrow, L., & Chou, V. (Eds.) (2008). *Improving literacy achievement in urban schools: Critical elements in teacher preparation.* Newark, DE: International Reading Association.
This volume provides ways to design and improve professional development for teachers in urban settings, by not only addressing the curricular and pedagogical challenges urban educators face but also by providing practical information for improving professional development and teacher preparation.

Xu, S. (2010). *Teaching English language learners: Literacy strategies and resources for K-6.* New York: Guilford.
Substantially based in research and knowledge of classroom practice, this volume shows K-6 teachers how to support ELLs. It includes ideas for

teaching across different grade and proficiency levels, such as ways to link instruction to students' lived experiences, using a variety of motivating print and electronic texts and materials, engaging families, and conducting effective assessments.

Zwiers, J. (2008.) *Building academic language: Essential practices for content classrooms.* New York: Wiley.
This volume discusses the functions and features of academic language that all teachers (language arts, history, mathematics, and science teachers) should know about (especially for ELLs) for supporting academic reading, writing, and discussion, including both instruction and assessment.

Glossary*

agglutinative   describing a language in which words are easily separated into their separate segments with separate grammatical functions

agreement   a relation between elements, in which a form of one word requires a corresponding form in the other

article   a member of the determiner lexical class marking either definite or indefinite

bootstrapping   in development, using what one knows to learn more

case marking   the form of a word that makes explicit its relation to other parts of a sentence, e.g., *her*, marking objective case in *I saw her in town*

classifier   typically refers to a form marking a noun and accompanied by a numeral

code switching   moving in speech between two languages or dialects

constructivism   theory of development that gives children a role in determining the paths their development takes

false friend   a word in one language sounding like one in a different language and mistakable as having the same meaning

family, language   a group of languages developed from a common ancestor

generic   a term referring to a whole class of entities rather than individuals

govern   linking one word to another such that the former requires a certain grammatical form of the other

grammar   a systematic account of the structure of a language

---

* The glossary was prepared with the assistance of Crystal, D. (1980). *A first dictionary of linguistics and phonetics*. London: Andre Deutsch; and Matthews, P. H. (2007). *Oxford concise dictionary of linguistics* (2nd ed.). Oxford: Oxford University Press.

head the part of a unit that determines the syntax of the unit

marked having a feature as opposed to its absence, e.g., in English, the plural is typically marked, the singular unmarked

morpheme the smallest unit of a language that signals meaning
    bound an element that attaches to a root to change or add meaning, e.g. *-s*
    free an element that stands alone, e.g., a word

morphology the study of how, or the ways that, words are structured

morphosyntactic referring to the morphological and syntactic features of units, such as number and case

particle an invariable word not falling into any traditional parts of speech

phoneme the smallest distinctive unit of a language

phonology the study of the sound system of a language

pitch the perceptual property of sound corresponding to the physical property of frequency

polyglot speaking or writing several languages, or a person who does so

pragmatics the study of meaning in context

pro-drop (subject dropping) the dropping of subjects of sentences that some languages allow; also sometimes referred to as the *null subject parameter*

register (stylistic) a set of language features used in speech or writing for a particular purpose or by a particular group, often to distinguish it socially

scaffolding, discourse providing support for learning through conversation

schwa name given to a neutral, unstressed vowel

semantics the study of meaning in a language

stress a feature of sound whereby one syllable is heard as more prominent than others

syllable a phonological unit that can be pronounced in isolation, usually larger than a single sound

syntax the study of grammatical relations between words and other units in sentences of a language

typology, language the study of language similarities and differences

universal a property or feature claimed to be common to all languages

References

Aud, S., Hussar, W., Kena, G., Frohlich, L., Kemp, J., & Tahan, K. (2011). *The condition of education 2011* (NCES 2011–033). US Department of Education, National Center for Education Statistics. Washington, DC: US Government Printing Office.

August, D., Goldenberg, C., Saunders, W. M., & Dressler, C. (2010). Recent research on English language and literacy instruction. In M. Shatz & L. C. Wilkinson (Eds.), *The education of English language learners* (pp. 272–297). New York: Guilford.

Bailey, A. L. (2008). Assessing the language of young learners. In E. Shohamy & N. Hornberger (Eds.), *Encyclopedia of language and education* (2nd ed., Vol. 7, Language testing and assessment) (pp. 1–20). New York & Berlin: Springer.

Bailey, A. L. (2010). Implications for assessment. In M. Shatz & L. C. Wilkinson (Eds.), *The education of English language learners* (pp. 222–247). New York: Guilford.

Bailey, B. (2000). Language and negotiation of ethnic/racial identity among Dominican Americans. *Language in Society, 29*, 555–582.

Beck, I., McKeown, M., & Kucan, L. (2003). Taking delight in words: Using oral language to build young children's vocabularies. *American Educator, 27*(1), 36–46.

Berman, R. A. (2007) Developing linguistic knowledge and language use across adolescence. In E. Hoff & M. Shatz (2007). *Blackwell handbook of language development* (pp. 347–367). Oxford, UK: Blackwell.

Berman, R. A. (2008). The psycholinguistics of developing text construction. *Journal of Child Language, 35*, 735–771.

Best, C. T. (1994). The emergence of native-language phonological influences in infants: A perceptual assimilation model. In J. C. Goodman & H. C. Nusbaum (Eds.), *The development of speech perception: The transition from speech sounds to spoken words* (pp. 167–224). Cambridge, MA: MIT Press.

Bialystok, E. (1999). Cognitive complexity and attentional control in the bilingual mind. *Cognitive Development, 70*, 636–644.

Bialystok, E. (2011). How analysis and control lead to advantages and disadvantages in bilingual processing. In C. Sanz & R. Loew (Eds.), *Implicit and explicit language learning: Conditions, processes, and knowledge* (pp. 49–58). Washington, DC: Georgetown University Press.

Bowerman, M. & Choi, S. (2001). Shaping meanings for language: Universal and language-specific in the acquisition of spatial semantic categories. In M. Bowerman & S. Levinson (Eds.), *Language acquisition and conceptual development* (pp. 475–511). Cambridge, UK: Cambridge University Press.

Bransford, J., Brown, A., & Cocking, R. (Eds.) (1999). *How people learn: Brain, mind, experience, and school.* Washington, DC: National Academy Press.

Brisk, M. E. (2006). *Bilingual education: From compensatory to quality schooling.* Mahway, NJ: Erlbaum.

Brisk, M. E. (2010). Learning English as a second language. In M. Shatz & L. C. Wilkinson (Eds.), *The education of English language learners* (pp. 152–176). New York: Guilford.

Brown, A. & Campione, J. (1994). Guided discovery in a community of learners. In K. McGilly (Ed.), *Classroom lessons: Integrating cognitive theory and classroom practice* (pp. 229–270). Cambridge, MA: MIT Press.

Brown, A. & Palincsar, A. (1987). Reciprocal teaching of comprehension strategies. In J. D. Day & J. G. Borkowski (Eds.), *Intelligence and exceptionality: New directions for theory, assessment, and instructional practice* (pp. 81–132). Norwood, NJ: Ablex.

Bruner, J. (1986). *Actual minds, possible worlds.* Cambridge, MA: Harvard University Press.

Carle, E. (1987). *The Very Hungry Caterpillar.* New York: Putnam.

Cary, S. (2004). *Going graphic: Comics at work in the multilingual classroom.* Portsmouth, NH: Heinemann.

Cazden, C. (1988). *Classroom discourse: The language of teaching and learning.* Portsmouth, NH: Heinemann.

Chamot, A. (2009). *The CALLA Handbook: Implementing the Cognitive Academic Language Learning Approach.* New York: Allyn & Bacon.

Clinton, H. R. (1996). *It takes a village: And other lessons children teach us.* New York: Simon & Schuster.

Conboy, B. T. (2010). The brain and language acquisition: Variation in language knowledge and readiness for education. In M. Shatz & L. C. Wilkinson (Eds.), *The education of English language learners* (pp. 25–47). New York: Guilford.

Cummins, J. (2000). *Language, power, and pedagogy: Bilingual children in the crossfire.* Buffalo, NY: Multilingual Matters.

Danzak, R. L. (2011). Defining identities through multiliteracies: ELL teens narrate their immigration experiences as graphic stories. *Journal of Adolescent and Adult Literacy,* 55(3), 187–196.

Danzak, R. L. & Silliman, E. (2005). Does my identity speak English? A pragmatic approach to the social world of an English language learner. *Seminars in Speech & Language,* 26(3), 1–15.

Danzak, R.L., Wilkinson, L. C., & Silliman, E. (2012). Cultural-linguistic diversity and inclusion. In J. Arthur & A. Peterson (Eds.), *The Routledge companion to education.* Abingdon, UK: Routledge.

DeAvila, E. A. & Duncan, S. E. (1991). *Language assessment scales.* San Rafael, CA: Linguametrics.

Dunn, J., Brown, J., Slomkowski, C., Tesla, C., & Youngblade, I. (1991). Young children's understanding of other people's feelings and beliefs: Individual differences and their antecedents. *Child Development,* 62, 1352–1366.

Earle-Carlin, S. & Hildebrand, C. (2000). *American perspectives: Readings on contemporary US culture.* New York: Pearson.

Echevarria, J., Vogt, M., & Short, D. (2000). *Making content comprehensible for English language learners: The SIOP Model.* Boston: Allyn & Bacon.

Eeds, M. & Wells, D. (1989). Grand conversations: An exploration of meaning construction in literature study groups. *Research in the Teaching of English,* 23(1), 4–29.

Englert, C. S., Tarrant, K. L., Mariage, T. V., & Oxer, T. (1994). Lessons talk as the work of reading groups: The effectiveness of two interventions. *Journal of Learning Disabilities*, 27, 171–175.

Faltis, C. & Coulter, C. (2008). *Teaching English learners and immigrant students in secondary schools.* New York: Allyn & Bacon.

Fisher, D., Frey, N., & Rothenberg, C. (2008). *Content-area conversations: How to plan discussion-based lessons for diverse language learners.* Alexandria, VA: Association for Supervision & Curriculum Development.

Gaskins, I., Rauch, S., Gensemer, E., Cuicelli, E., O'Hara, C., Six, L., & Scott, T. (1997). Scaffolding the development of intelligence among children who are delayed in learning to read. In K. Hogan & M. Pressley (Eds.), *Scaffolding student learning: Instructional approaches and issues* (pp. 43–73). Cambridge, MA: Brookline Books.

Gavelek, J. & Raphael, T. (1996). Changing talk about text: New roles for teachers and students. *Language Arts*, 73, 182–192.

Gawande, A. (2010). *The checklist manifesto: How to get things right.* New York: Metropolitan Books.

Goetz, P. (2003). The effects of bilingualism on theory of mind development. *Bilingualism: Language and Cognition*, 6, 1–15.

Goldenberg, C. & Patthey-Chavez, C. (1995). Discourse processes in instructional conversations: Interactions between teacher and transition readers. *Discourse Processes*, 19, 57–73.

Goldin-Meadow, S. (2003). *The resilience of language: What gesture creation in deaf children can tell us about how all children learn language.* New York: Psychology Press.

Hamayan, E. & Perlman, R. (1990). *Helping language minority students after they exit from bilingual/ESL programs.* Washington, DC: National Clearinghouse for Bilingual Education.

Harvey, S. & Daniels, H. (2009) *Comprehension and collaboration: Inquiry circles in action.* Portsmouth, NH: Heinemann.

Haviland, J. (2011). Action, gesture, and grammar: Iconicity in Zinacantec family homesign. Colloquium, Department of Anthropology, University of Michigan, Ann Arbor, MI (November 14, 2011).

Help! They don't speak English: A resource guide for educators of limited English proficient migrant students: Grades pre-K-6 (1998, 3rd ed.). Arlington, VA: AEL.

Hoff, E. (2009). *Language development* (4th ed.). Belmont, CA: Wadsworth.

Hoff, E. & Shatz, M. (Eds.) (2007). *Blackwell handbook of language development.* Oxford, UK: Blackwell.

Hogan, K. & Pressley, M. (1997). Scaffolding scientific competencies within classroom communities of inquiry. In K. Hogan & M. Pressley (Eds.), *Scaffolding student learning: Instructional approaches & issues* (pp. 74–107). Cambridge, MA: Brookline Books.

Hudson River Center (1999). *Native language literacy screening device.* Glenmont, NY: Hudson River Center for Program Development.

Humes, K., Jones, N., & Ramirez, R. (2011). Overview of race and Hispanic origins: 2010. Washington, DC: US. Department of Commerce, Economics and Statistics Administration, US Census Bureau. Retrieved from: www.census.gov/prod/cen 2010/briefs/c2010br-02.pdf.

Irwin, D. & Bushnell, I. (1980). *Observational strategies for child study.* Belmont, CA: Wadsworth.

Kovacs, M. & Mehler, J. (2009). Cognitive gains in 7-month-old bilingual infants. *Proceedings of the National Academy of Sciences*, 106(16), 6556–6560.

Kuczaj, S. (1983). *Crib speech and language play*. New York: Springer.

Levy, C. (2011). My family's experiment in extreme schooling. *New York Times*. September 18, 2011.

Lipson, M. & Wixson, K. (2010). *Successful approaches to RTI: Collaborative practices for improving K-12 literacy*. Newark, DE: International Reading Association.

Lucy, J. (1992). *Grammatical categories and cognition: A case study of the linguistic relativity hypothesis*. Cambridge, UK: Cambridge University Press.

Markman, E. M. (1991). The whole-object, taxonomic, and mutual exclusivity assumptions as initial constraints on word meanings. In S. A. Gelman & J. P. Byrnes (Eds.), *Perspectives on language and thought: Interrelations in development* (pp. 72–106). Cambridge, UK: Cambridge University Press.

Martinez, I. (2000). The effects of language on children's understanding of agency and causation. Unpublished dissertation, University of Michigan, Ann Arbor, MI.

Matthews, P. H. (2007). *The concise Oxford dictionary of linguistics* (2nd ed.). Oxford, UK: Oxford University Press.

Nelson, K., Denninger, M., Bonvillian, J., Kaplan, B., & Baker, N. (1984). Maternal input adjustments and non-adjustments as related to children's linguistic advances and to language acquisition theories. In A. D. Pellegrini & T. Yawkey (Eds.), *The development of oral and written languages: Readings in developmental and applied linguistics* (pp. 31–56). New York: Ablex.

Nelson, K., Welsh, J., Trupp, E., & Greenberg, M. (2011). Language delays of impoverished preschool children in relation to early academic and emotion recognition skills. *First Language*, 31, 164–194.

Ogle, D. (1986). K-W-L: A teaching model that develops active reading of expository text. *Reading Teacher*, 39, 564–570.

Paradis, J. (2007). Second language acquisition in childhood. In E. Hoff & M. Shatz (Eds.), *Blackwell handbook of language development* (pp. 387–405). Oxford, UK: Blackwell.

Pauk, W. (2001). *How to study in college 7/e*. Boston: Houghton Mifflin Company.

Pearson, B. Z., Fernandez, S. C., & Oller, D. K. (1993). Lexical development in bilingual infants and toddlers: Comparison to monolingual norms. *Language Learning*, 43, 93–120.

Penn, D., Holyoak, K., & Povinelli, D. (2008). Darwin's mistake: Explaining the discontinuity between human and nonhuman minds. *Behavioral and Brain Sciences*, 31, 109–130.

Polka, L., Rvachew, S., & Mattock, K. (2007). Experiential influences on speech perception and speech production in infancy (pp. 153–172). In E. Hoff & M. Shatz (Eds.), *Blackwell handbook of language development*. Oxford, UK: Blackwell.

Pressley, M. & Woloshyn, V. (Eds.), (1995). *Cognitive strategy instruction that really improves children's academic performance* (2nd ed.). Cambridge, MA: Brookline Books.

Provonost, P. & Vohr, E. (2010). *Safe patients, smart hospitals: How one doctor's checklist can help us change health care from the inside out*. New York: Hudson Street.

Reyes, I. & Ervin-Tripp, S. (2010). Language choice and competence: Code switching and issues of social identity in young bilingual children. In M. Shatz & L. C. Wilkinson (Eds.), *The education of English language learners* (pp. 67–86). New York: Guilford.

Roehler, L. R. & Cantlon, D. J. (1997). Scaffolding: A powerful tool in social constructivist classrooms. In K. Hogan & M. Pressley (Eds.), *Scaffolding student learning: Instructional approaches and issues* (pp. 6–42). Cambridge, MA: Brookline Books.

Rogoff, B. (1990). *Apprenticeship in thinking: Cognitive development in social context.* New York: Oxford University Press.

Rymes, B. (2010). *Communicative repertoires and English language learners.* In M. Shatz & L. C. Wilkinson (Eds.), *The education of English language learners* (pp. 177–198). New York: Guilford.

Saffran, J. R. & Thiessen, E. D. (2007). Domain-general learning capacities. In E. Hoff & M. Shatz (Eds.), *Blackwell handbook of language development* (pp. 68–86). Oxford, UK: Blackwell.

Shatz, M. (1987). Bootstrapping operations in child language. In K. E. Nelson & A. van Kleeck (Eds.), *Children's language: Vol. 6* (pp. 1–22). Hillsdale, NJ: Erlbaum.

Shatz, M. (1991). Using cross-cultural research to inform about the role of language in development: Comparisons of Japanese, Korean, and English, and of German, American English, and British English. In M. Bornstein (Ed.), *Cultural approaches to parenting* (pp. 139–154). Hillsdale, NJ: Erlbaum.

Shatz, M. (1994). *A toddler's life: Becoming a person.* New York: Oxford University Press.

Shatz, M. (2007a). On the development of the field of language development. In E. Hoff & M. Shatz (Eds.), *Blackwell handbook of language development* (pp. 1–15). Oxford, UK: Blackwell.

Shatz, M. (2007b). Revisiting *A toddler's life* for *The toddler years*: Conversational participation as a tool for learning across knowledge domains. In C. Brownell & C. Kopp (Eds.), *Socioemotional development in the toddler years* (pp. 241–257). New York: Guilford.

Shatz, M., Diesendruck, G., Martinez, I. B., & Akar, D. (2003). The influence of language and socioeconomic status on children's understanding of false belief. *Developmental Psychology*, 13, 39–71.

Shatz, M., Dyer, J., Massaro, D., & Marchetti, A. (2006). Culture and mental states: A comparison of English and Italian versions of children's books. In A. Antonietti, O. Liverta Sempio, & A. Marchetti (Eds.), *Theory of mind and language in different developmental contexts* (pp. 93–106). New York: Springer – Science & Business Media.

Shatz, M. & Ebeling, K. (1991). Patterns of language learning related behavior: Evidence of self-help in acquiring grammar. *Journal of Child Language*, 18, 295–313.

Shatz, M. & Gelman, R. (1977). The development of communication skills: Modifications in the speech of young children as a function of listener. *Monographs of the Society for Research in Child Development*, 38(5), 1–37.

Shatz, M. & McCloskey, L. A. (1984). Answering appropriately: A developmental perspective on conversational knowledge. In S. Kuczaj (Ed.), *Discourse development* (pp. 19–36). New York: Springer-Verlag.

Shatz, M., Tare, M., Nguyen, S. P., & Young, T. (2010). Acquiring non-object terms: The case for time words. *Journal of Cognition and Development*, 11, 16–36.

Shatz, M. & Wilkinson, L. C. (Eds.) (2010). *The education of English language learners: Research to practice.* New York: Guilford.

Siegal, M., Kobayashi, F., Surian, L., & Hjelmquist, E. (2011). Theory of mind and bilingual cognition. In V. Cook & B. Bassetti (Eds.), *Language and bilingual cognition* (pp. 431–452). London: Psychology Press.

Silliman, E., Bahr, R., Beasman, J. & Wilkinson, L. C. (2000). Scaffolds for learning to read in an inclusion classroom. *Language, Speech, and Hearing Services in Schools*, 31, 265–279.

Silliman, E. & Wilkinson, L. C. (1991). *Communicating for learning*. Gaithersburg, MD: Aspen Publications.

Silliman, E. & Wilkinson, L. C. (Eds.) (2007). *Language and literacy learning in schools*. New York: Guilford.

Silliman, E. & Wilkinson, L. C. (2010). Literacy. In P. Hogan (Ed.), *The Cambridge encyclopedia of the language sciences* (pp. 448–450). Cambridge, UK: Cambridge University Press.

Slavin, R. E., Madden, N., Calderón, M., Chamberlain, A. & Hennessy, M. (2011). Reading and language outcomes of a five-year randomized evaluation of transitional bilingual education. *Educational Evaluation and Policy Analysis*, 33, 47–58.

Spelke, E. (2003). What makes us smart? Core knowledge and natural language. In D. Gentner & S. Goldin-Meadow (Eds.), *Language in mind: Advances in the study of language and thought* (pp. 277–311). Cambridge, MA: MIT Press.

Stone, C. A. (1998). The metaphor of scaffolding: Its utility for the field of learning disabilities. *Journal of Learning Disabilities*, 31, 344–364.

Swan, M. & Smith, B. (Eds.) (2001). *Learner English*. Cambridge, UK: Cambridge University Press.

Tamir, Y. (2011). Staying in control; or, what do we really want public education to achieve? *Educational Theory*, 61(4), 395–411.

Terrace, H., Petitto, L., Sanders, R. J., & Bever, T. (1979). Can an ape create a sentence? *Science*, 206, 891–902.

Tharp, R. (1994). Research knowledge and policy issues in cultural diversity and education. In B. McLeod (Ed.), *Language and learning: Educating linguistically diverse students* (pp. 129–167). Albany, NY: State University of New York Press.

Thomas, M. & Karmiloff-Smith, A. (2005). Can developmental disorders reveal the component parts of the human language faculty? *Language Learning and Development*, 1, 65–92.

Thomas, W. & Collier, V. (1997). *School effectiveness for language minority students*. National Clearinghouse for English Language Acquisition (NCELA) Resource Collection Series, No. 9.

Valenzuela, A. (1999) *Subtractive schooling: US–Mexican youth and the politics of caring*. Albany, NY: State University of New York Press.

Verplaetse, L. & Migliacci, N. (Eds.), (2008). *Inclusive pedagogy for English language learners: A handbook of research-informed practices*. New York: Lawrence Erlbaum Associates, Taylor & Francis Group.

Vygotsky, L. (1978). *Thought and language*. Cambridge, MA: MIT Press.

Weir, R. (1962). *Language in the crib*. Ann Arbor, MI: University of Michigan Press.

Whaley, L. (1997). *Introduction to typology: The unity and diversity of language*. Thousand Oaks, CA: Sage.

Wilkinson, L. C. & Silliman, E. (2000). Classroom language and literacy learning. In M. Kamil, P. Mosenthal, P. Pearson, & R. Barr (Eds.), *Handbook of reading research, Vol. III* (pp. 337–360). Mahwah, NJ: Erlbaum.

Wilkinson, L. C. & Silliman, E. (2008). Academic language proficiency and literacy instruction in urban settings. In L. C. Wilkinson, L. Morrow, & V. Chou (Eds.),

Improving literacy achievement in urban schools: Critical elements in teacher preparation. Newark, DE: International Reading Association.

Wilkinson, L. C. & Silliman, E. (2010). Academic language proficiency. In C. Clauss-Ehlers (Ed.), *Encyclopedia of cross-cultural school psychology* (pp. 573–576). New York & Berlin: Springer-Verlag Publishers.

Wilkinson, L. C. & Silliman, E. (2012). Language. In J. Arthur & A. Peterson (Eds.), *The Routledge companion to education.* Abingdon, UK: Routledge.

Wilkinson, L. C. & Spinelli, F. (1983). Using requests effectively in peer-directed instructional groups. *American Educational Research Journal,* 20(4), 479–501.

William, D. (2006). Commentary: Formative assessment: Getting the focus right. *Educational Assessment,* 11(3–4), 283–289.

Wimmer, H. & Perner, J. (1983). Beliefs about beliefs: Representations and constraining function of wrong beliefs in young children's understanding of deception. *Cognition,* 13, 103–128.

Wolf, M., Wilson, E., Rapp, D., Waite, K., Bocchini, M., Davis, T., & Rudd, R. (2009). Literacy and learning in health care. *Pediatrics,* 124, Supp 3, S275–281.

Wong Fillmore, L. & Snow, C. (2000). What teachers need to know about language. ERIC Clearinghouse on Language and Linguistics. Retrieved August 1, 2000 from www.cal.org/ericc11.

Yang, G. (2006). *American Born Chinese.* New York: First Second Books.

Zwiers, J. (2004). The third language of academic English. *Educational Leadership,* 62(4), 60–63.

Zwiers, J. (2008). *Building academic language: Essential practices for content classrooms.* New York: Wiley.

Index